GUITAR WORLD PRESENTS

STEVIE RAY. IN HIS OWN WORDS.
The tragic and inspiring inside story of
the legendary blues guitarist. Featuring penetrating
interviews, in-depth guitar lessons and
reminiscences by the artists who knew him best.

From the pages of
GUITAR WORLD
magazine

Edited by
**Jeff Kitts, Brad Tolinski
and Harold Steinblatt**

Published by Music Content Developers, Inc.
In cooperation with Harris Publications, Inc. and Guitar World Magazine
Guitar World is a registered trademark of Harris Publications, Inc.
Exclusively Distributed by

HAL•LEONARD®
CORPORATION
7777 W. BLUEMOUND RD. P.O. BOX 13819 MILWAUKEE, WI 53213

787.
8716
GUI

ISBN 0-7935-8080-3
Copyright © 1997 Music Content Developers, Inc.
600 Valley Road, Suite 206, Wayne, NJ 07470

Executive Producer: Brad Tolinski
Producer: Carol Flannery
Editors: Jeff Kitts & Harold Steinblatt
Art Director: John Flannery
Cover Photo: Jonnie Miles
Editorial Photos: Ebet Roberts

Table of Contents

GUITAR WORLD, DECEMBER 1990

THE GOOD TEXAN

The musical life of Stevie Ray Vaughan, who rose from obscurity to become a blues titan.

By Bill Milkowski

H E WAS, PERHAPS, the greatest blues guitarist of his generation. Stevie Ray Vaughan, who died in a helicopter crash after performing live on August 27, 1990—just 36 days short of his 36th birthday—played with blistering, note-bending intensity, a gut-wrenching vibrato and tons of soul. His all-too-abbreviated legacy—five albums as a leader and a number of powerful sideman stints—ended with a long-overdue collaboration with older brother Jimmie Lee Vaughan, on the posthumously released 1990 album, *Family Style*. A well-balanced mixture of driving rock and roll, smooth r&b, earthy funk and heartfelt blues, the album took SRV full circle, back to his South Dallas days, paying tribute to the music the Vaughan boys listened to and loved in the Sixties and Seventies.

Stevie Ray Vaughan was born October 3, 1954, the son of Big Jim and Martha Vaughan. Brother Jimmie, three-and-a-half years his senior, exerted an early influence on SRV via his record collection, which included albums by such disparate guitar stylists as Jimmy Reed, Freddie, Albert and B.B. King, Kenny Burrell, Albert Collins, Charlie Christian and Django Reinhardt.

Stevie first picked up the guitar in 1963, at the age of eight. "I wanted to play drums, but I didn't have any drums," he recalled in a 1984 interview. "Then I wanted to play saxophone, but all I could get out of it was a few squeaks.

"My big brother played guitar, so I figured I'd try it, too. He would leave his guitars around the house, and tell me not to touch them. That's basically how I got started—sneaking into his room and playing his guitars. It didn't take me any time to figure out that that was what I wanted to do."

Stevie's first electric guitar—a gift from Jimmie—was a hollow-body Gibson Messenger. From there he graduated to a 1952 Fender Broadcaster—another hand-me-down from his older brother. By then, SRV had purchased his first record, a copy of Lonnie Mack's instrumental hit, "Wham," which, along with several Albert King records, were the prime sources from which Stevie Ray shaped his own approach to the instrument.

In 1968 he bought a '54 black Les Paul TV model and joined his first band, an r&b outfit called Blackbird, which patterned itself after two of Stevie Ray's favorite acts of the day, Hank Ballard & the Midnighters and Johnny G & the G-Men.

Shortly after joining Blackbird, he purchased a '52 Les Paul Gold Top with soapbar pickups, and began playing with schoolmate Tommy Shannon in a band called The Chantones. He also occasionally played bass in brother Jimmie's band, Texas Storm.

The following year saw Stevie—perhaps owing to the towering influence of Jimi Hendrix—procure his first Stratocaster, a '63 model with a maple neck. He played the Strat as a member of Cast of Thousands, a band he joined while in high school. A rare sample of the 16-year-old Stevie's playing exists on *A New Hi*, a 1971 compilation album of local Dallas bands, which includes a track by Cast of Thousands.

By late 1969 Jimmie had moved to Austin, drawn to the burgeoning blues scene centered around the Vulcan Gas Company, the nightclub where, a year earlier, Johnny Winter had recorded his *Progressive Blues Experiment* album. Longtime Stevie Ray-friend Mike Kendrid recalls:

"In those days in Dallas, you either played the hits or you didn't play. So there was kind of a mass exodus of blues lovers from Dallas—me, Jimmie, Stevie, Paul Ray. We all eventually came to Austin, because the musical climate was so much more open to blues and originals."

Jimmie played those "blues and originals" in Storm, a gutsy trio that included future Fabulous Thunderbirds bassist Keith Ferguson, and was soon renowned in Austin for his guitar playing and comprehensive knowledge of blues and r&b. Stevie dropped out of school and joined the exodus to Austin in the spring of 1972. Some time later he fell in with Crackerjack, which featured Johnny Winter's rhythm section—drummer Uncle John Turner and bassist Tommy Shannon. That summer also marked the first time he saw Albert King—who was to become his single biggest influence—perform live.

"I had a gig somewhere else that night," remembered Stevie years later. "After a quick set I got on the microphone and said, 'Ladies and gentlemen, I don't know about you, but I'm gonna go see Albert King, and if you have any brains, you will too.' Then I just packed up and left.

"By the time I got to Albert's gig, there were only about 75 people left in the place. I ended up standing on a table right beside the stage, just staring at him throughout the whole set. Part way through the show he took his mic stand and walked over to where I was standing, planted it, and just stood there and sang and played to me the rest of the night. He didn't know me from Adam. I was just this skinny little kid, 98 pounds soaking wet. I guess I must've yelled, 'Right!' or something. And when he finished playing, he walked over to me, handed me his guitar and shook my hand. I was stunned. I'll never forget it."

Three-and-a-half years later, on stage at Antone's, Little Stevie Vaughan (as he had come to be known) realized the thrill of jamming with the great man himself. "First thing he did was walk up to me and point his finger, saying, 'I remember you—we met about three-and-a-half years ago.' It's amazing, but he never forgets people. And later that night, he called me up on stage to play. I thought

I was going to do one song with him, but I ended up playing the rest of the night."

Writer Brad Buchholz recalled that magical night at Antone's in his Dallas Morning News tribute to SRV: "The skinny kid in hip-hugger bell-bottoms and downcast eyes blew away gruff old Albert King that night. At one point, Mr. King stepped away from Little Stevie and hid his guitar behind the stage curtains, as if to say, 'This little kid is scaring my guitar.' "

In the spring of 1973 Little Stevie left Crackerjack to join the Nightcrawlers, a popular local r&b outfit. By then, blues and r&b had supplanted the outlaw country rock of Willie Nelson and Waylon Jennings as Austin's reigning sound. One of the most happening nightspots at the time was the One Knite, a cramped bar which, as a club T-shirt proclaimed, was "the dive where all your dreams come true." The Knite showcased the best local bands on weeknights, among them Jimmie Vaughan and Texas Storm (Mondays) and Mark Benno and the Nightcrawlers, with Little Stevie Vaughan (Wednesdays). Longtime SRV fan Margaret Moser-Malone wrote in her Austin Chronicle appraisal of those days:

"The Nightcrawlers looked like their name sounded—a motley, surly crew of musicians that included Drew Pennington on harp and vocals, Keith Ferguson on bass, Doyle Bramhall on drums, Stevie on guitar and assorted others who drifted in and out of the band. I must have been 19 or 20; Stevie would have been around 19, too. It was a good time to be young and in love with the blues. I lived for nights at the One Knite. And I especially lived for seeing Stevie Vaughan in the Nightcrawlers. I was absolutely galvanized by his performances on that tiny stage…"

By 1973 Stevie had traded his '63 maple neck Strat for a '59 rosewood fingerboard model, which remained his number one guitar for the rest of his career. (In a bizarrely portentous accident, the neck of his beloved '59 was snapped in two pieces on July 9 of 1990, when a huge piece of scenery at the Garden State Arts Center in New Jersey crashed onto a number of SRV's guitars.)

Little Stevie left the Nightcrawlers at the end of 1974, and became the second guitarist, alongside Denny Freeman, with the Cobras. "Stevie's first gig with the band was New Year's Eve 1975," recalls Cobra vocalist and leader Paul Ray. "I had known him and Jimmie from back in Dallas when they were just kids. I remember seeing Stevie play bass in Jimmie's band when he was 14 years old. Then when Stevie came to town, it didn't take long before everybody was talking about this skinny little guitar player. I was glad to get him in my band, and lucky that he stayed for two years. What can you say? He was great."

During SRV's tenure with the Cobras, the band cut a 45 that was released regionally. One side, "Texas Clover," featured Denny Freeman on lead guitar, while the flip side, "Other Days," showcased Stevie's lightning Strat work. The smoking guitar tandem helped the Cobras gain a fanatical following around Austin. It was with this band that Stevie Ray began his singing career.

"I was sitting in the audience at a little club downtown on Congress Avenue called After Hours," recalls Austin guitarist Van Wilks. "I was checking out Stevie with the Cobras. Then, all of a sudden, Stevie starts singing that Freddie King song, 'Goin' Down,' and I nearly fell off my chair. Everybody knew he was a great guitar player, but nobody had ever heard him sing before. Later, he developed his voice into a phenomenal instrument, even though he remained kind of shy about it. Hendrix said he didn't like his own voice, either, and I always felt he had an incredible singing voice. I thought the same thing about Stevie. I mean, there was more to him than just playing single notes on the guitar."

Two significant events jolted the Austin scene almost simultaneously: Jimmie Vaughan formed the Fabulous Thunderbirds, and Clifford Antone opened a blues haven on 6th Street. As the club owner recently recalled, "I had an import clothing store, and in a big ol' room in back we had amps and drums and a PA set up for late-night jam sessions. I'd play bass, Jimmie and Stevie played guitar, Doyle Bramhall played drums—just a bunch of friends jamming the blues from seven in the evening until four, five in the morning. When the city passed the 2 a.m. drinking bill *[bars had previously been forced by law to close by midnight*] we just found a building and opened up the nicest club this town's ever seen."

By the summer of 1977 Stevie had left the Cobras to form Triple Threat Revue, a versatile outfit featuring Mike Kendrid (composer of "Cold Shot") on piano, W.C. Clark on vocals and bass, Dallas drummer Freddie Pharaoh and the fiery Fort Worth vocalist Lou Ann Barton, who left the T-Birds to join Stevie's new band. What with Stevie's Hendrix covers, Lou Ann's torch ballads and Janis Joplin covers, and W.C.'s Freddie King covers, the band was indeed a Triple Threat. Ultimately, however, egos clashed. As the Austin American Statesman's blues maven Michael Point put it, "Lou Ann really wanted a guy to back her up on guitar, and not show her up with guitar hero tricks. And Stevie wanted a back-up vocalist, not a star. That tension was often visible on stage."

The conflict didn't prevent Stevie from including Lou Ann in the original line-up of Double Trouble (named after his favorite Otis Rush song), which he formed in May of 1979. Cleve Hattersley, an Austin musician who moved to New York in 1978, recalls booking that first edition of Double Trouble in 1980, at the old Lone Star in Manhattan. "We booked them for $100. They drove all the way up from Austin and crashed on friends' couches. The gig went all right, but afterward, Lou Ann kind of got out of hand. She was real drunk, and threw beer glasses and screamed at the waitresses. And Stevie, of course, was upset. That was the final gig that band ever had together."

By 1981 Stevie had streamlined Double Trouble down to a power trio that featured Crackerjack bandmate Tommy Shannon on bass and Chris Layton on drums. It was also right around this time that he began calling himself Stevie Ray. The revamped group, with its clear emphasis on Stevie Ray's toe-curling, Albert King-styled blues-power and Hendrixian histrionics, was a big hit back home at Austin blues joints like the Rome Inn, Antone's and The Continental Club. SRV was, perhaps, at the peak of his guitar powers, and was locked in a friendly, unofficial competition with Eric Johnson for rights to the title, "Austin Guitar God."

Word of Austin's hometown hero eventually reached the great r&b producer Jerry Wexler, who flew to Texas in 1982 to catch Stevie Ray on his home turf. Considerably impressed with the guitarist's talents, Wexler used his influence to place Double Trouble on the bill at the 1982 Montreux Jazz Festival in Switzerland—a coup almost unheard of for an unsigned act. Stevie Ray's stinging Strat licks were well-received by his European audience. Particularly impressed by the Texan's fiery fretboard work was David Bowie. After Double Trouble's set, Bowie met with Stevie Ray to raise the possibility of the guitarist appearing on his next album. Bowie eventually hired Stevie Ray to play on *Let's Dance* and appear on his 1983 world tour. SRV cut the tracks, layering the funky, Nile Rodgers-produced grooves with some fine Albert King-style licks. But he didn't make the tour. Apparently, one stipulation of the deal was that while Double Trouble would open the Bowie shows, Stevie Ray could discuss his playing with the press only in the context of the David Bowie show—not his own band's. There were also rumors of a financial dispute between the two parties. SRV pulled out of the tour and returned to Austin to play the bars with Double Trouble.

"It was a real Texas thing to do," said Michael Point of the Austin American Statesman. "Basically, Stevie Ray said, 'Fuck you, Mr. Bowie. We're sticking to our guns.' And that individualistic stance earned Stevie Ray big points with the Texans. They were proud of him for standing up for his music, and not being pushed around by some British rock star."

It wasn't long before opportunity came knocking once more on Stevie Ray's door. Jackson Browne, a fan since his own encounter with Vaughan at the 1982 Montreux Festival, offered him the use of his Down Town studio, to record a demo that hopefully would land Double Trouble a record contract. The taped results of Double Trouble's labors in Browne's studio made their way to John Hammond Sr., the legendary talent scout and producer, who counted Charlie Christian, Bob Dylan, Aretha Franklin and Bruce Springsteen among his many discoveries. Excited by Stevie Ray's fresh take on an old formula, Hammond purchased the demo and used his industry clout to secure a deal for Double Trouble with Epic Records.

In an interview conducted with Hammond soon after Stevie Ray was signed, the producer spoke glowingly of his find. "The first great Texas guitar player I ever saw in the flesh was T-Bone Walker, back in 1936. And Stevie Ray is in that great tradition. He has such a direct quality. And he's a great showman, too, just like T-Bone was."

The music on Stevie Ray's first album, *Texas Flood*, was full of fire. The rough-hewn texture to the rhythm guitar parts on "Pride and Joy" and "I'm Crying," two Vaughan originals, established the thick-toned Texas shuffle as an SRV trademark. His solos were laced with an intensity and sense of abandon that often triggered visceral responses from audiences. And there was the flamboyance: silk scarves and leopard coats, ponchos, Indian headdresses and cowboy boots, not to mention his penchant for playing the guitar behind his neck and with his teeth. This was Stevie Ray Vaughan, the quintessential Texas Strat burner.

It was clear from the outset that Stevie Ray was no media-hyped charlatan. Not only was he thoroughly grounded in the work of the classic electric blues masters—his solos reflected the influence of players from every walk of blues life—but his playing was imbued with the kind of spirit and honesty that could only signify the real deal. He drew on skills honed in tough Texas nightclubs, and it showed in the integrity of his playing. While he was true to himself, he at the same time never failed to give credit where it was due. In a 1988 interview, he noted:

"Nowadays it seems that no matter what you do, it's already been done. It must've been a wonderful thing to come along at a time when electric blues was developing as an American music form. To those guys like T-Bone and Muddy, Hubert Sumlin, Jimmy Rogers, Lightnin' Hopkins, Buddy Guy, Albert King, B.B. King and Freddie King and a bunch of others, it must've been a free, free feeling to make this kind of music. And they deserve respect for being the innovators—those guys are the ones who really ought to have the recognition."

Texas Flood peaked at 38 on the *Billboard* album charts, and sold more than 500,000 units in 1983. Stevie Ray received Grammy nominations for Best Rock Instrumental (the lightning Texas boogie of "Rude Mood") and Best Traditional Blues (the deep blues of "Texas Flood").

In 1984 *Couldn't Stand the Weather* was released, along with a video—Stevie Ray's first—made for the title cut. The typically Texas-macho clip received moderate airplay on MTV. This wider exposure helped push the album to platinum and further cemented Stevie Ray's status as the reigning Texas Guitar King. As he continued to forge his own identity on slightly-behind-the-beat Texas shuffles like "Cold Shot" and "Honey Bee," he simultaneously pursued the ghost of Jimi Hendrix, much to the delight of his young fans. If the connection was not apparent from his version of Guitar Slim's "The Things That I Used to Do" (rendered as a kind of response to Jimi's "Red House"), it became clear to one and all with Stevie Ray's near-faithful rendition of "Voodoo Chile (Slight Return)," which became a concert favorite.

Organist Reese Wynans joined Double Trouble in 1985, giving the band the bigger, beefier sound it projected on *Soul to Soul*. Stevie continued dogging Jimi's shadow with "Say What!" his answer to Hendrix's "Rainy Day Dream Away," and on Earl King's "Come On," a tune Hendrix covered on Electric Ladyland. Stevie Ray kept the Texas shuffles chugging along with "Lookin' out the Window" and "Look at Little Sister." And he kept dipping heavily into the Albert King bag, particularly on the slow blues of "Ain't Gone 'n' Give Up on Love" and the gospel-tinged "Life without You." The album attained Gold status. It also served to confirm Vaughan's status as the legitimate heir of Jimi Hendrix, at least in the eyes of the generation that came of age after Jimi's death.

In some ways, he truly was that heir. "It just seemed like Hendrix was always in his thoughts," said Austin guitarist Van Wilks. "He was certainly in his heart and fingers. I remember one time we were talking about Hendrix—which is where our conversations would always ultimately lead—and I pulled this picture of Jimi's tombstone from my wallet, which I'd taken when I was playing a gig in Seattle. I found out that Jimi was buried in Renton, Washington, so I went there to pay my respects. Anyway, when I showed Stevie Ray this picture, his eyes just got so wide—he couldn't believe it. He just stood there and held that picture in his hand, and stared at it for a long time."

On the surface, Stevie Ray's life was as rosy a success story as one could hope to find. Inside, however, was another matter: The guitar hero was running scared. Substance abuse had seriously clouded his vision, and was beginning to hurt his playing.

Constant road work and grueling late-night mixing sessions for the double *Live Alive* album helped run Stevie Ray into the ground. He remained on schedule by staying up for days on end—and by ingesting all the cocaine he could get his hands on. Finally, in the early part of October 1986, he collapsed on stage at a performance in London. Instinctively, he called his mother back home in Dallas with a plaintive S.O.S.: "Help. I'm over here in Europe somewhere, and I'm in real bad shape."

He returned to the United States a few days later. On October 17, he entered a detox center in Marietta, Georgia, where he remained through November. Upon his release, he returned to Dallas in an effort to escape the drugs, alcohol and late-night hanging out that plagued him in Austin.

After openly acknowledging his alcoholism, Stevie Ray determinedly tackled Alcoholics Anonymous' 12-step program. By 1988 he was back on the road with renewed vigor, playing with more conviction and clarity than ever before. His walk on the sober side paid off with 1989's *In Step*, his strongest, most focused project up to that time. The album went Gold, and won a Grammy for Best Contemporary Blues Recording.

Stevie Ray took a breather from recording *Family Style* in Memphis for a brief return to his old stomping grounds, and to attend the eighth annual Austin Music Awards. The event could easily have been called the "SRV Awards," for the guitarist was named Musician of the Decade, and came away with honors for Record of the Decade (*Texas Flood*), Record of the Year (*In Step*),

Single of the Year ("Crossfire") and Musician of the Year. Clad in understated formal attire, he expressed his gratitude to the capacity crowd at Palmer Auditorium.

"I just want to thank God that I'm alive. And I want to thank all the people that loved me back to life so that I could be here with you today."

GUITAR WORLD, SEPTEMBER 1983

BEFORE THE FLOOD

From the roadhouses of Austin comes
Stevie Ray Vaughan, riding his Stratocaster
to blues greatness on TEXAS FLOOD.

By Frank Joseph

PRESENCE—THE ABILITY to make direct, emotional contact with a listener's heart—is that elusive intangible for which all guitarists strive and few attain. Stevie Ray Vaughan, Texas blues man, has presence to spare. His razor-edged guitar impacts emotionally on David Bowie's space-age funk opus, *Let's Dance*, and simultaneously on Vaughan's debut album, *Texas Flood* (Epic), and firmly establishes him in the fertile ranks of Lone Star blues masters.

Just slightly more than a year ago Vaughan was known only in barrooms across Texas, where his band, Double Trouble—drummer Chris Layton, guitarist Johnny Winter and veteran bassist Tommy Shannon—plied their special brand of blues. From that dead-end roadhouse existence, Stevie's gut-wrenching vibrato and intense, machine-gun delivery began catching the ears of some important people. Two noted juke-joint prowlers, Rolling Stones Mick Jagger and Keith Richards, caught Double Trouble at a Dallas club and flew the band up to New York to play at a private party. The Stones expressed interest in signing Double Trouble to their RS label, though they never followed through with a contract. But when Stones roll, they make waves. Noted producer and talent-hunter Jerry Wexler arranged a move that proved to be, both literally and figuratively, a giant step for Stevie's guitar-led group.

"Jerry had heard us in an Austin club," Vaughan explains, "and he contacted the director of the 1982 Montreaux Jazz Festival and got us booked there." The invitation to appear was a double honor, as Double Trouble became, on the strength of Wexler's recommendation, the first act ever to perform at Montreaux without an album.

Though Stevie Ray was a bit intimidated by Montreaux's heavyweight line-up—"We weren't sure how we'd be accepted"—the searing licks that emanated from his array of classic Stratocasters won over the international audience. And any lingering doubts Vaughan may have had were alleviated by a request from David Bowie.

"As soon as we were finished," Stevie says of his introduction to rock's Man of a Thousand Faces, "someone came backstage and told us David Bowie wanted to meet us." The English art rocker and Texas blues trio headed over "to the musician's bar at the casino," Vaughan details, "where we talked for hours. We ended up playing at the bar for several nights, and Jackson Browne came in and jammed with us."

As it turned out, Bowie was preparing to record an "underlying r&b work," and with some persistence hired Stevie to play lead on *Let's Dance* and in his band for his current world tour. Since the first of the year Bowie has made a point of informing the music media that "Stevie is the most exciting city blues stylist I've heard in years." Going a step further, Bowie has placed Double Trouble on the bill for his outdoor U.S. concerts, insuring the widest possible exposure for Vaughan.

Jackson Browne, whose interest wasn't quite so vested as Bowie's, offered Stevie his Down Town studio to record an album that would win Double Trouble a record deal. The LP was presented to the legendary producer John Hammond Sr., whose greatest discoveries—Count Basie, Charlie Christian, Bob Dylan, Aretha Franklin, Bruce Springsteen—are all groundbreakers in the pantheon of American popular music. "Immensely excited" by Vaughan's "freshness," Hammond purchased the album, *Texas Flood*, and signed Double Trouble to the CBS-distributed label bearing his name. From his Manhattan office, the music industry's most respected maven remarks, "I was so delighted by Stevie's sound—it's unlike anyone else's—and he's such a marvelous improviser, never repeating exactly the same thing twice." In addition, Hammond was impressed by the band's "strong ensemble sense."

That "sense" is a result of Vaughan and company's having performed almost nightly since Double Trouble was formed in May, 1979. In order to preserve the band's symbiotic intensity, *Texas Flood* (except for some of the vocals) was recorded live in the studio, without overdubbing or headphones. Vaughan's insistence on this point led to a most unusual occurrence, which underscores the trio's precision.

"In the middle of one of the tunes I broke a string and we had to stop," Vaughan recalls. "After I changed the string we picked up right where we left off—and punched back in at the same time. I don't know if this has ever been done before. The engineer sort of looked at us weird, but we got it on the first take." Stevie laughs, refusing to reveal the song's title, challenging listeners to guess for themselves.

Hammond personally took the role of executive producer for *Texas Flood*. "There was a strange balance, and we spent a lot of time remixing it," he says. It is a job he obviously relished, however. "I can't take too much credit for Stevie. He came to me, and that's almost unique in my experience. Only one other person has done that—Bruce Springsteen—and that's pretty good company."

Hammond has in his career been intimately involved with the development of such guitar giants as Eddie Lang, Charlie Christian and George Benson. Of this rather select group, he states, "They are all on the highest possible plateau, and Stevie's right up there with them. There's nothing artificial about his presence—it's honest music." Drawing an analogy between two of the celebrated guitarists and Vaughan, Hammond comments, "Charlie came in and gave Benny [*Goodman*] new life, and I think Stevie's doing the same for David Bowie. Eddie Lang was a trailblazer in the Twenties and Thirties, and Stevie's a trailblazer in the Eighties. He's the true kind of creative force that one looks for but rarely finds. He's truly original, and I automatically compare him to Robert Johnson because Stevie's got that unique passion."

Passion for the blues and the guitar's presence is a family tradition for Vaughan, whose brother Jimmie, the excellent guitarist for the Fabulous Thunderbirds, was a strong role model during their childhood in a Dallas suburb. "I wanted to play saxophone, but all I could get were a few squeaks," remembers Stevie, who first picked up a guitar in 1963. "So, my big brother was playing guitar and I figured I'd try it, too."

Loving it from the get-go, Stevie progressed from "a cardboard copy of a Roy Rogers" to his first electric model and amp, a hollow-body Gibson Messenger and a Silvertone. The Silvertone was soon supplemented by a Fender Champion 600. Vaughan remarks, "I had the right kind of amps from the beginning."

Within a year, Stevie was exposed to the classic licks of B.B., Freddie and Albert King, Albert Collins and other electric blues masters "on the records Jimmy brought home." As his interest in the guitar inflamed, Stevie began pestering his brother for lessons. "Jimmie showed me a lot of stuff," the younger Vaughan credits, "but there was a time when he warned, 'If you ask me to show you anything again, I'll kick your ass.' Well, I did and he did!"

Also at this time, Stevie heard the blistering guitar instrumental "Wham," by Lonnie Mack, whose supercharged lines and tone heavily influenced Vaughan's mature style.

"Lonnie was ahead of his time, but at the same time he was right in there with Albert Collins' 'cool sounds.' "

Sixteen years later Vaughan had the thrill of meeting his guitar hero. "Lonnie came into an Austin club where we were playing. I asked him if he would play, but Lonnie, the master of the Flying V, said he wouldn't touch anything but a Gibson [*Vaughan's arsenal was all vintage Strats*], and so he just got up and sang his ass off. Later he said he wanted to produce us."

By 1966 Vaughan was trying his first Fender guitar, a '52 Broadcaster he borrowed from his brother Jimmie. Two years later, at 14 (and now using a black '54 Les Paul TV model, again supplied by his brother), Stevie joined his first full-time band, Blackbird. Shortly after joining Blackbird, which had a strong following on the Dallas club circuit, Stevie purchased a '52 gold-top Les Paul.

Today a confirmed "Fender man," who is the proud owner of four classic Stratocasters, Vaughan says of the Gibson solid-bodies: "I never dug regular Les Pauls with that dirty sound, though I liked Jimmie's TV model because it was real clear. The '52 sounded good, too, because it had whistlers [*Gibson "soapbar" pickups*] and not humbuckers, which I'd never use." If not quite a Les Paul fan, Stevie has come to appreciate "the better Gibson hollow-bodies. I had a Barney Kessel that I got 11 years ago that I really enjoyed until 1975, when it was ripped off, and now there's my '59 dot-neck 335." Vaughan appreciates the dot-neck 335 because "it sounds and feels pretty. It has a real strong bass response, and at the same time it's real bright." Concerning the prized neck, he says, "All dot-necks are different; mine's not too thin or big around like a log. But it's wide, which is important because I have big hands, and it fits me real well."

In 1969 Vaughan purchased his first Stratocaster, a '63 maple-neck. He began absorbing Jimi Hendrix's epochal, blues-rooted guitar explorations, at the same time frequenting black venues to experience traditional r&b players first hand. Recalls Stevie, "Blackbird, though basically an r&b band, played all-white clubs. But between sets I'd sneak over to the black places to hear blues musicians. It got to the point where I was making my living at white clubs and having my fun at the other places." Stevie's fun was derived from seeing fine local acts like Big Boy and the Arrows and established virtuosos like B.B. and Albert King, Albert Collins, Buddy Guy, Bobby "Blue" Bland with Wayne Bennet and Howlin' Wolf with Hubert Sumlin—"the same people I'd go see now if they were still around."

Stevie is quick to cite Magic Sam, Otis Rush and his brother Jimmie as prime influences, but perhaps more than any other guitarist, Jimi Hendrix left the most indelible mark on Vaughan's playing. "I love Hendrix for so many reasons," he states with great reverence. "He was so much more than just a blues guitarist—he played damn well any kind of guitar he wanted. In fact I'm not sure if he even played the guitar—he played music."

Vaughan was not particularly pleased with the Stratocaster he bought in 1969. "It was constantly giving me trouble and driving me nuts," he says of the '63 maple-neck. So, for the remainder of his high school years, he switched "back and forth between the '52 and '54 Les Pauls, and the '52 Broadcaster," before settling on the Gibson Barney Kessel hollow-body in 1972.

Following high school Stevie relocated to Austin, a city blossoming with music opportunities. On a return gig to Dallas in 1973 with his new band, the Nightcrawlers, Vaughan arranged a trade for what would become the most important guitar he ever owned.

"I walked into this guitar store carrying my '63 Strat," he recalls, "and I saw this other Strat hanging in the window. I just had to have it—I hadn't even played it, but I knew by the way it looked it sounded great—and I asked if they wanted to trade." The "new" guitar—Stevie's prize '59 rosewood Stratocaster—became his main axe from the moment he acquired it.

Though Vaughan calls the Strat "my '59," the guitar's true age is somewhat unclear. "It was officially put out in 1962," he explains, "but the neck is stamped '59. When I got it there was a sticker under the bass pickup that read 'L.F. '59.' So I think Leo Fender put it together with spare parts and issued it in '62. But it doesn't really matter to me; all I know is that I've never found another one that sounds like it."

One spare part Stevie is especially fond of is the rosewood neck. "The neck is shaped differently from most others. It's a D-neck, but it's oddly shaped—it's real, real big, and fits my hand like a glove."

"My yellow '64 is very strange," is how Stevie describes another of his beloved Strats. "It was owned by the lead guitar player for Vanilla Fudge, who trashed it by putting four humbuckers in it. Charley Wirz [*of Charley's Guitar Shop in Dallas*] gave it to me a couple of years ago, and I had him fix it up and put one stock treble Fender pickup in it. The body rings like a bell because it's practically hollow—the middle was cut out for the humbuckers—and the only part that's solid is the edge." Vaughan used his "bell-like" Strat to record "Tell Me," from *Texas Flood*.

Stevie left the Nightcrawlers in 1973 to take the guitar chair in the Cobras, a long-established, Austin-based r&b band. Two years later, he helped form Triple Threat, with whom he played "as much r&b as I could pull off." Patterned after an r&b revue, Triple Threat featured an unusual line-up that included five lead singers, among them Stevie himself. In early 1978 the band folded, and with Triple Threat singer Lu Ann Barton he organized Double Trouble, named after his favorite Otis Rush song.

As may be discerned from *Texas Flood*, Double Trouble is decidedly not a power trio in the conventional sense. Vaughan's guitar dominates the sound. "Lots of times I'll play lead and rhythm together," he says. "I play as many different things—piano, sax and harp parts—as I can at once. Whatever I can fit, whenever I need to."

A hallmark of Stevie's playing is its broad-ranging, tasteful versatility. The glass-breaking vibrato, torrid showers of licks, driving chords and occasional feedback have managed to please both hardcore blues purists and high-energy rock fans, a circumstance obviously not lost on David Bowie.

"I don't know what kind of music you'd call it," says Stevie of Bowie's album, "but I tried to play like Albert King and it seemed to fit."

Vaughan's description is a bit too modest. While he relied more on his King-like wailing vibrato than on his arsenal of hot licks, it is very doubtful whether Albert King and his Flying V could have so seamlessly fit into Bowie's work. Like two of his heroes, Lonnie Mack and Jimi Hendrix, Vaughan has successfully integrated blues guitar in music far removed from the style's original contexts. That is what John Hammond refers to as Stevie's "freshness."

The truly killer aspects of Vaughan's playing are his fat tone and full-bodied clarity, which combined constitute one of the most formidable sounds in guitardom. Stevie Ray attributes his power to his picking technique, string setup and equipment. "Most people can't bend my strings," he states matter-of-factly. "The gauges I'm using now—.013, .016, .019, .028, .038, .056—are small for me, but if I use 'em any bigger, I tear my fingers off." Vaughan also has a habit of tearing his frets off. "The way I play, I go through a set in a year. So I put '58 Gibson Jumbo Bass frets on all my necks." To facilitate string-bending Vaughan tunes his guitar to E flat.

Stevie has over the years searched for the right combination of amplifiers and speakers. His quest will end "as soon as I get enough money to buy a Dumble. I can't say enough good things about those amps." Stevie used Jackson Browne's Mother Dumble to record *Texas Flood*. Meanwhile, Vaughan employs a Marshall Combo with two 12-inch JBLs and two Fender Vibraverbs, no. 5 and 6, with one 15-inch JBL. "My amps are backwards," he laughs. "I use the Fenders for distortion and the Marshall for clarity." He adds, "The Marshall is supposed to be 200 watts, but mine's never worked right; it peaks out at 80."

On stage Stevie uses only one Fender head, as he runs a Y cord from his guitar to the Marshall and one of the Vibraverbs, an obscure 50-watt amp which Fender marketed in the early Sixties. The other Fender serves as a speaker cabinet.

For Bowie's album, Vaughan played through a rented post-CBS Super Reverb; for the tour, he says, he "just bought two Mesa Boogies. I don't even know what models they are—they're the small wooden ones. The reason I'm using them is they sound a lot like a Dumble. But that doesn't mean I'm not going to buy a Dumble as soon as I get the money!"

All of Vaughan's guitars have stock pickups. He occasionally employs two devices, an Ibanez Tube Screamer and Vox wah-wah pedal, to beef up his sound. "I use the Tube Screamer because of the tone knob," he says. "That way you can vary the distortion and tonal range. You can turn it on slightly to get a Guitar Slim tone, which is how I use it, or wide open so your guitar sounds like it should jump up and bite you." None of the devices were used for *Let's Dance*. The Tube Screamer did its dirty work on two *Texas Flood* cuts: the title track and, in conjunction with the wah-wah, "Testify."

Equipment aside, one of the most crucial elements of Vaughan's sound is the way he uses his fingers. "Sometimes I slide 'em, rubbing the sides of the strings," he explains. "To get a big, fat sound that punches out I pop the strings with either my second or third finger. Usually I'll hold the pick but ignore it, and get my second or third finger under the string, pull it and let go. Basically, it's what modern bass players do—it gives me a real bright, poppier tone. But now I can get that same tone with my thumb, just by laying into the string a little harder." Here Vaughan pauses to laugh at himself. "But like my brother Jimmie says, I play like I'm breaking out of jail anyway."

GUITAR WORLD, NOVEMBER 1985

SOUL MAN

Stevie Ray Vaughan looks deep into the r&b well and discovers—himself.

By Bruce Nixon

OMETHING WAS UP. Stevie Ray Vaughan looked like the cat that swallowed the canary. He had plenty of reasons to be pleased: A few weeks earlier Vaughan and his band, Double Trouble, had received their first Grammy Award (in the ethnic music category, for some tunes on a Montreux Jazz Festival blues anthology), capping a year in which they'd won a number of other industry awards. After seeing their first two albums climb into the upper reaches of the charts, Stevie Ray and his band toured widely at home and abroad, and were at that moment in the midst of finishing up work on their third album, *Soul to Soul*.

But it was obvious that something more than a year of new triumphs and successes was on Stevie Ray's mind, as he was being deliberately and playfully vague. He positively seemed to glow.

Was he born again?

"Something like that." There was a faint wisp of a knowing smile under his broad-brimmed hat.

Quit drinking and smoking?

He held up his glass. "No."

Make up with his wife or family over something?

"That's part of it."

Vaughan grinned mischievously, and talk moved in other directions. He was sitting in the dim corner of a lounge in a pleasant North Dallas hotel, waiting to leave for the studio where *Soul to Soul* was coming down the home stretch. A little later, the rest of the band—drummer Chris Layton and bassist Tommy Shannon—came down, and they clearly possessed something of the same glow. Was this contagious?

"Yeah, some big changes have taken place. I haven't resolved all my problems," Vaughan explained, "but I'm working on it. I can see the problems, at least, and that takes a lot of the pressure off. I've been running from myself too long, and now I feel like I'm walking with myself."

It is understood by many who know him that Stevie Ray Vaughan was at first uncomfortable with his sudden success, perhaps a bit bewildered by it—and not entirely prepared for its accompanying responsibilities. He was confused by those people who gravitated to him because of his success, and not because of him or his music.

Despite all that's happened to him during the past two years or so, Vaughan projects not so much as the slightest aura of rock stardom. He seems very much the hard-working club player he used to be—friendly, modest, down-to-earth. He chuckled at the memory of playing Austin clubs years ago, making a few dollars for the night and then borrowing money from the bartender to cover the bar tab—he remembered that $1.36 was the least he'd ever earned on a paying gig. Now he's a success, and at some point he finally began to understand it all. He's getting used to the attention, the star-gazers and the paparazzi.

Vaughan spoke at great length of his current album, and about some of his plans for the immediate future. He was very excited about the new Lonnie Mack album, which he co-produced (and played on) in Austin last year. He'd picked up a few important life lessons from the veteran guitarist; Mack, of course, has seen and done it all in his long career, and lived with and without success.

He smiled: "I sat down and talked to the man—he's one of

those men who will sit down and talk to you. And thank God for that. He's a wonderful cat. He opened my eyes to a lot of things."

While touring in Australia recently, Double Trouble crossed paths with Eric Clapton, another player who has worked hard to come to grips with the implications of his enormous success.

"He didn't tell me what to do," Vaughan said. "He told me how it'd been for him." Clapton and Vaughan holed up in a hotel room for a few hours, reflecting on the good life and its pitfalls.

"Then we were working with Albert King, and he came up to me and said, 'Man, we got to sit down and have a little heart-to-heart.' You sit down like that with Albert King and you grow."

And Vaughan remembered something that came from Johnny Winter, the first white Texas blues guitar hero, who'd preceded him down the long path.

"He said something to me when the first record was doing so well," Stevie Ray recalled. "It made me feel a lot of respect for what we did, for the music. He said that he wanted me to know that people like Muddy Waters and the cats who started it all really had respect for what we're doing, because it made people respect them. We're not taking credit for the music. We're trying to give it back."

A few weeks later, when I talked to Vaughan again, he elaborated on his relationship with Albert King. It was almost midnight, a warm Dallas spring night, and we were driving across the northwest part of the city, looking for hamburgers while rough mixes of the new album played on the tape deck. "Albert calls me his godson," Vaughan said. "He's pleased with what we've done, and he explained some simple things: Don't get high when you're working, because you're having too much fun and you don't see the people screwin' you around. Have fun—that's great—but pay attention.

"That happened when things were happening so fast, and it was real important to hear that kind of stuff. He knows. He's been through it. You wake up one day back in the clubs, without a whole lot to show for what you've been through."

Talk turned back to Lonnie Mack. "He's something between a daddy and a brother," Vaughan explained. "When he sees something that needs to be talked about, he'll talk. He understands. He's real deep—a warm kind of deep. He wanted to produce us three years ago, but it didn't happen then, and things just worked out like they have. The way I look at it, we're just giving back to him what he did for all of us. It wasn't a case of me doing something for him—it was me getting a chance to work with him.

"You know," he added, "it's wonderful the way people come into your life when you need them, and it happens in so many ways. It's like having an angel. Somebody comes along and helps you get right."

Vaughan, Shannon and Layton can barely contain their excitement about the new record. Stevie Ray wanted to make a buoyant record, he said, with shorter songs, less heavy breathing from the guitar, and some new instrumental combinations. *Soul to Soul* is filled with Stevie Ray Vaughan trademarks, but it has a good-time, uptown feel—a strong trace of r&b—that distinguishes it from Vaughan's first two albums. The guitar showpieces are there, but it's clear that Vaughan set out to accomplish something different with this record.

"There are a lot of rockin' songs," he said, "and then some like we've never played before. There's definitely blues in it—not less blues than before—but it's a type of music we haven't really tried before, some different kinds of changes. There are a few other players here and there that people won't expect. Some keyboards [*ex-Delbert McClinton pianist Reese Wynans has been added to Double Trouble*], some horns. But the moods are happier."

At that particular time, the band was working nightly at Dallas Sound Lab, a 48-track, digitally-capable facility in the Dallas Communications Complex at Las Colinas, just northwest of the city. They'd booked the studio in great 24-hour chunks of time, and even recorded rehearsals. Vaughan was finding the conditions pretty luxurious—one benefit of having two successful albums under his belt. It helped shape the character of the music on the new record.

"It's helping a lot," Vaughan explained, "because we've gotten to work on individual technique and things, we've come down to playing more like we wanted to play in the first place. To do that, we had to cut in the studio and then sit down and listen to it. Before, we were always forced to work a lot faster than this. And we play so many gigs on the road that we don't have the time to listen to ourselves as closely as we should. You go and play for an hour and a half and then go to the next place, and you don't get a chance to catch what's changing in your music, what's working and what isn't working. We love to play shows—don't misunderstand me—but it's hard to pick up on whether or not we've improved. We have fun when we play live, but the studio is a blessing that a lot of people forget about."

He remarked that he and Double Trouble were recording the album the "old way"—live, in the same room together, and without headphones. "I've got every amp I own in the studio, all going all-out at once," Vaughan laughed. "They had to build a new monitor system for us." The studio, he explained, was set up like a stage, with the amps positioned so that the other players could hear what was coming out of them. Vaughan even played drums on one cut, but as the track was too slow, it was speeded up.

"We're recording the old way and using the best modern equipment we can find; it's a good combination," Vaughan said. "We go in and cut a song a few times if we need to, or just do a set. At this point, we're pretty fine-tuned, and we're watching it grow as it goes. We're all examining everything. We have a lot of ideas, things we've wanted to have a chance to work with."

Double Trouble toured for 18 1/2 months prior to the 1984 release of *Couldn't Stand the Weather*, and then took two months off before starting the new project. "We didn't realize how hard it was to just go play cold, without having played in front of people. I'd never thought about that before. We'd rehearse—try to play this and that—but we didn't play in front of people. You'd be amazed how hard it is not to play in front of people."

In any case, you don't get the sense that a lot of career planning goes into a Double Trouble album—no big calculations about how it should sound or how many units it should sell. What's charted, mainly, is the growth of Vaughan and the band:

"We're trying for feeling. We try to accomplish something with the music, which is to feel through things. I've been trying to grow up some myself, in my heart, and it's happening quick. I feel good about it, and I want that to come out in the music."

Meanwhile, Vaughan remains—like many Texas guitarists—a die-hard Stratocaster player who uses a minimum of effects. For the new album, he's stuck mostly with the white, Strat-style guitar he posed with for the cover of *Couldn't Stand the Weather*. Built in 1983 for Vaughan by his friend, the late Dallas guitar dealer and repairman Charley Wirz, the guitar features Danelectro pickups and custom wiring. The instrument's sound is exemplified by the light, quickly strummed break in "Tin Pan Alley Blues," which was recorded with only a low Leslie effect.

A simple message is engraved on the metal plate where the neck joins the body on the back of the guitar: "To Stevie From Charley. More In '84." It's rather characteristic of the generous spirit that Vaughan's early success inspired in many of his old Texas fans—indeed, *Soul to Soul* is dedicated to Wirz.

"I've been going between that guitar, the beat-up '59 Strat and this other guitar that Charley found for me, a '61 Strat," said Vaughan. "It's brutal. They all have that neck, and I associate them with Charley—I didn't get the '59 from him, but he worked on it so many times that it feels like I did, I guess. I like the white one. It sounds like my old beat-up one, but it's cleaner, not quite as full-sounding. And Charley never told anybody but me what he did when he wired it.

"But that's the sound," he added. "That Leslie and that guitar, if the amp's working clean. You have to use the right amp, like a Super, with the Leslie and a Vibraverb head—it's really a steel guitar head. If you set 'em all up in a live room, it sounds great. I don't use a chorus—I like to get that sound with a Leslie, too. It's old-fashioned, but I'm trying to bring it up-to-date."

Vaughan is fairly vague about his amp setup, though he admits to keeping two Vibraverbs, two Super Reverbs, a Dumble 150-watt

Steel String Singer (which he'd stopped using for a while, but returned to recently) and the Leslie all hooked together. The actual combination, he explained, was determined over a period of time by which amp worked when, until he accidentally came up with a combination that he liked.

Other amps seem to come and go—indeed, in the several weeks between interviews, he'd acquired another Fender. "They're hooked up pretty straight, I guess," he grinned. "I have a Tube Screamer, a wah and the Leslie on my pedal board, and an on-off switch for everything, so that when I switch it off, between the guitar and amp there ain't nothin'. When I do a song like 'Third Stone from the Sun,' I can't control the feedback with the effects on. It goes crazy, so I switch 'em all off and then kick it back when I'm done. It's mostly straight, though—a weird setup—but pretty straight." In addition to that, he continues to play with his guitar tuned a half-step low—"E-flat tuning" he calls it—and he said that before Wirz died earlier this year, they had discussed building a custom-scale neck that would allow Vaughan to use the tuning without transposing with concert-pitch instruments. It sounds like an impossible idea, but who knows? When two stone guitar fools like Stevie and Charley got together, anything was possible.

Vaughan's use of the low-pitch tuning was Hendrix-inspired, in any case. "He did it a lot," said Stevie Ray. "It gives you different overtones. It's an interesting sound, and I find it a lot easier to sing to." He's also acquired the wah-wah pedal used by Hendrix to record "Up from the Sky."

He speaks without any self-consciousness about Hendrix, with whom he has often been compared. In May, Vaughan played a solo version of "The Star Spangled Banner" at the Houston Astros' home opener at the Astrodome. Immediately, people recalled the world-weary, apocalyptic version played by Hendrix at Woodstock in 1969. And the performance triggered yet a new round of comparisons between Hendrix and Stevie.

"I heard they even wrote about it in one of the music magazines," said Vaughan. "They tried to put the two versions side by side.

I hate that stuff. His version was great."

And yet, the comparison exists—if only because Vaughan includes at least one or two (and sometimes three) Hendrix songs in each live show, because he featured a well-known Hendrix song ("Voodoo Chile") on his second album, and most of all, perhaps, because he captures the spirit of the improvisational Hendrix on stage more accurately than any other contemporary guitarist.

An affinity obviously exists. In Texas, Vaughan is regarded by his old crowd as a hot blues player with a tight band and a lot of rock and roll in his sound; the blues variations are still common in Texas clubs. His music has been refined and expanded by all the work and opportunities that have come his way in the past two or three years, but at its core, it's still the steamy, torrid blues he played in the late Seventies. The people outside Texas—those less familiar with his story, who know his work only from records and the hype of the last few years—have turned Vaughan's long-standing love for Hendrix's work into a point of comparison. Vaughan himself feels it's all been overplayed.

According to one person in his organization, Vaughan labored long and hard over the decision to add "Voodoo Chile" to *Couldn't Stand the Weather*, and that he finally decided to include the song because he felt that his younger audience hadn't heard Hendrix, and he wanted to spread the word.

"I loved his music, and I feel like it's important to hear what he was doing, just like anybody else, like Albert, B.B. or any of that stuff," Vaughan remarked. "I wanted to do the song, but I didn't want to mistreat it. I try to take care of his music, and it takes care of me. Treat it with respect, not as a burden—like you have to put a guy down because he plays from it. That's crazy. I respect him for his life and his music."

At a Dallas show in late April, Vaughan used the Wirz Strat and the '59 and, when a string broke on that guitar, a custom Hamilton. On slow blues like "Tin Pan Alley," the white guitar had a thin, edgy, cutting sound, sweet but hard. The '59 Strat is a fuller, chunkiersounding guitar, more of a rocker, more typical of the thick tones on *Couldn't Stand the Weather*; it is Vaughan's instrument of choice when he does Hendrix covers.

While they weren't airing many new tunes that night—it was a free concert with Lonnie Mack, in front of a hometown crowd—Double Trouble were debuting their new keyboard player, Reese Wynans, who appears on *Soul to Soul*. Vaughan himself played beautifully that night: His slow blues remain vehicles for gorgeous displays of phrasing and tone, and he has a growing arsenal of tricks and techniques, from his flowing, syncopated strum ("Pride and Joy") to funky, overstated string-snapping effects. In the past two years, he's learned a lot about working an audience as well. In the clubs he was a straightforward, stand-up player. Today he's a good showman as well.

"Getting that passion," says Stevie Ray, "that's what I try to do."

Within days of the Dallas date, the new Lonnie Mack album, *Strike Like Lightning* (Alligator), finally hit the stores; it was the first record from the legendary guitarist in some seven years. While Vaughan downplays his role as co-producer—it's his first production effort outside Double Trouble—it's clear enough from the handful of guitar duels included on the album that Vaughan helped create a heck of a guitar album. Vaughan, of course, has always acknowledged Mack's influence on his own playing—"Wham!" was the first single he ever owned—and the two hit it off wonderfully when they finally began working together. The empathy and interplay is obvious.

Vaughan remembered the first time he met Mack. It was 1978 or '79, and an earlier version of Double Trouble (without Layton) was playing in a club in Austin when Mack walked in. "I was playing the second chord of 'Wham!' that night when he came through the door," said Vaughan. "We did the shit outta 'Wham!' It was cookin'. And there was Lonnie Mack. At first, I didn't even recognize him. Man, it was like magic."

At the time, Mack was assembling a new road band, and he approached Vaughan about joining him. That never came to pass, of course, but the two remained friends over the years. When

Alligator signed Mack in mid 1984, Mack and Alligator president Bruce Iglauer talked to Vaughan about producing the record, and he agreed instantly.

"They were his tunes, and I just tried to help him with what he wanted to do with the record; that's what I think producing is," Vaughan said. "A lot of producing is just being there, and with Lonnie, just reminding him of his influence on myself and other guitar players. Most of us got a lot from him. Nobody else can play with a whammy bar like him: He holds it while he plays, and the sound sends chills up your spine. You can't do that with a Stratocaster. "I just didn't want to sound like I was trying to direct the record."

Things are moving pretty fast for Vaughan, but he has a feeling that this is only the beginning. The beginning wasn't David Bowie's *Let's Dance*, which helped showcase his work to the greater rock and roll public, or even *Texas Flood*, whose chart success seemed to surprise just about everyone, because of how far removed it was from the pop mood of that moment.

The beginning is now—this new attitude, the self-sustenance and self-reliance, the sense of faith in the future. What Vaughan stands to accomplish, perhaps, is an important service to the blues. The music is widely enough recognized as the foundation of rock and roll, but Vaughan may have the opportunity to bring the blues back into the current mainstream of rock in new ways, at a new level. He may, in fact—as Albert King has suggested—take the color out of the blues.

"I do feel as though I've grown as a player through all this," Vaughan remarked at one point. "It's funny—I'm trying to get back to how I used to play years and years ago, and yet, at the same time, to make those ideas grow, tie them into what we're doing now. I guess I'm just remembering where all these things come from. It's all pretty regular music to me, what I grew up with: the Glorytunes, Johnny G. and the G-Men. I used to hear some of those old bands in Dallas, at the Heights Theater in Oak Cliff, in '62 and '63.

"Now, I use heavy strings, tune low, play hard, and floor it." He laughed. "Floor it." Another chuckle. "That's technical talk."

GUITAR WORLD, DECEMBER 1986

THE HEART OF TEXAS

SRV gets out of rehab and gives a clearer perspective on his work.

By Andy Aledort

THIS CONVERSATION TOOK place in the hours before an SRV performance at the Mid-Hudson Civic Center in beautiful downtown Poughkeepsie, New York. I arrived at soundcheck time, 5:30 p.m., about two-and-a-half hours before the show. Unbeknown to me, Stevie had just been released from the hospital; the severe drug and alcohol addiction that nearly took his life had been kept very quiet. It had been about six weeks since he'd left the London rehabilitation clinic of Dr. Victor Bloom (who had previously helped Stevie's friend Eric Clapton to quit drinking), after which he checked into the Charter Peachford Hospital, in Atlanta, for a three-and-a-half week stay. This Poughkeepsie performance was just Stevie's eighth "dry" show.

Understandably, the backstage vibe was very tense, with Stevie's road manager barking orders at everyone. But when I finally sat down with Stevie, he was in good spirits, though his energy level was a bit low. He asked more than once to be excused for being "asleep," and asked if we could continue the interview later so that he could squeeze in a nap before showtime.

During the course of our post-show conversation, Stevie's good-humored banter was punctuated here and there with startlingly candid talk about his drinking problems. He did not appear to have any desire to "edit" himself in any way, shape or form. In fact, Stevie Ray spoke with the same clarity and directness that typically characterized his guitar playing.

STEVIE RAY VAUGHAN: It's one of those days, the sleepy kind. It's cold outside.

GUITAR WORLD: How was the Radio City Music Hall (New York City) show the other night?

VAUGHAN: Oh, it was fine. It was fun. Most of our equipment is falling apart. [*Stevie plugs in his main guitar, "Number One," and starts playing.*] Ooh, I'm outta tune!

GW: What year is that guitar?

VAUGHAN: 1959.

GW: How long have you had it?

VAUGHAN: I've had it for 13 years. I bought it around '73, I guess.

GW: Did it look like that when you got it, or did the previous owner treat it better than you do?

VAUGHAN: I don't treat it bad. It's just been around.

GW: Stevie, how did you first get started in music?

VAUGHAN: When I was real young, [*Western swing legends*] the Texas Playboys hung out at our house all the time. My parents played "42," and they'd come over and get drunk.

GW: What's "42"?

VAUGHAN: Dominoes. "42 to 84." Those guys hung around a lot, they'd do some playing, and we'd hear them play. Mainly, we'd hear them talking about playing. There were a lot of characters hanging around.

GW: Were [*Texas Playboy guitarists*] Eldon Shamblin or Junior Barnard among the guys who'd come over?

VAUGHAN: God, I don't remember their names. I was a little beefheart. [*laughs*] Every once in a while, my dad would yell [*speaks in heavy rural Texas accent*], "Hey, Jim, Steve, come out here and show them what you can do!" And we were little midgets, with guitars hangin' on us that were this big!

GW: How old were you when you first picked up the guitar?

VAUGHAN: Seven. The first guitar I had was one of those Roy Rogers guitars; it had pictures of cowboys and cows on it and some rope. I had a blanket that had the same shit on it, too.

GW: Did you sleep with the guitar and the blanket together?

VAUGHAN: Yeah! [*laughs*] I still sleep with my guitar when my woman ain't around!

GW: Do you remember the first records that you listened to?

VAUGHAN: Jimmie [*Vaughan, Stevie's older brother*] turned me on to a lot of different stuff. I remember him bringing home Hendrix, Buddy Guy, Muddy Waters, B.B. King. The first record I ever bought was "Wham," by Lonnie Mack, from 1963. "Wham" was a great record. I played it so many times that my dad smashed it! He got mad and broke it because I played it over and over and over and over. When I didn't think it could be any louder, I went and borrowed somebody's Shure Vocal Master PA, put mics in front of the stereo speakers, and then turned the PA up! It was loud in my room.

GW: And there went your records.

VAUGHAN: Not long after that. Every time he broke it, I just went and got another one.

GW: What did you pick up from listening to Lonnie Mack?

VAUGHAN: A lot of inspiration, I can tell you that. Between listening to that guy's feeling in his music and watching my brother, and how much feeling he had with it, I mainly just picked up big time inspiration. What I was getting out of it wasn't so much technical or anything—just the thought of them playing made me want to jump up and play.

GW: What were the bands Jimmie was playing in back in those early days?

SRV: He had several bands, such as the Swingin' Pendulums, and he was with Sammy Laurie and the Penetrations.

GW: What kind of music did these bands play?

VAUGHAN: It was rock and roll, rhythm and blues. He was always interested in all of that stuff. The Penetrations were also obviously into girls. [*laughs*]

GW: As in, penetrate your pants?

VAUGHAN: [*Stevie laughs so hard that he spits his coffee all over his pants*] Oh, shit! God damn! I'll be right back! [*He leaves to get cleaned up, and then returns.*]

GW: Besides Lonnie Mack, what were some of the other records you first played along with?

VAUGHAN: I was really into the Yardbirds—"Jeff's Boogie," of course. "Over Under Sideways Down." Lots of Hendrix. Clapton stuff with John Mayall. The Beatles were important. You know, get your Rickenbacker bass and go crazy playing "Lady Madonna," just like everybody.

GW: Did you listen to much T-Bone Walker?

VAUGHAN: Yeah. "T-Bone Shuffle," "Stormy Monday," "Cold, Cold Feeling." A lot of 'em I don't remember the names of; I just know the way they go. I had a bunch of his records.

GW: Were you listening to T-Bone before you heard Hendrix?

VAUGHAN: No, it was after, mostly. I listened to Hendrix first. See, I still listen to Hendrix, all the time—I doubt I'll ever quit.

T-Bone was the first guy to play behind his head, and on his back, on the floor. Those were all T-Bone tricks. And Guitar Slim.

GW: Did you listen to jazz guitarists like Kenny Burrell or Wes Montgomery?

VAUGHAN: Yeah, Kenny Burrell.

GW: "Gone Home," from *Soul to Soul*, is in that West Coast, Kenny Burrell style.

VAUGHAN: Yes, it is. We play "Chitlins con Carne" by Kenny Burrell [*the song appears on Stevie Ray's posthumous release,* The Sky Is Crying *(Epic, 1991)*].

GW: What other jazz guitar players did you listen to?

VAUGHAN: Wes Montgomery, a lot. Django Reinhardt. Grant Green. He's got some tone, man. Jackie King. Fred Walters. The Wes stuff is his recordings with trios and quartets. My favorite Wes record, for some reason, had an orchestra on it—it's called *In the Wee Small Hours*. God! Sometimes it sounds like muzak, but what he played on it...Kenny Burrell played rhythm guitar on it.

GW: Are there specific guitar things that you picked up from Wes?

VAUGHAN: I can't read music; I can't read a note. But every once in a while, I feel the "Wes" thing coming. I can't do it just sitting here. I've got to be groovin' out! [*Emits a huge yawn*] You'll have to excuse me today; I'm asleep. I haven't been stoned in a long time. I'm straight now. This is me straight, believe it or not. [*laughs*] It's 51 days today since I had a drink.

GW: How come?

VAUGHAN: Because I want to stop.

GW: How do you feel?

VAUGHAN: Lots better. Kinda crazy today, but I'm okay.

GUITAR WORLD, SEPTEMBER 1988

RESURRECTION

Stevie Ray Vaughan walks away from drugs and alcohol and is reborn in the blues.

By Bill Milkowski

STEVIE RAY VAUGHAN strides into the room, cutting a sharp figure with his signature snakeskin boots, gray *Late Night with David Letterman* T-shirt and cool black denim jacket, the back of which is emblazoned with the face of Dr. Martin Luther King Jr. And though time hasn't altered his taste in clothes much—five years ago, his look was similarly Texas-bohemian— there's a new air about the man, a palpably new vibe.

Gone are the bleary eyes and the tell-tale stagger. Gone is the booze-and-coke haze that hung over his eyes, his band, and his crew like a heavy shroud. A new, positive spirit permeates the entire entourage, from Stevie Ray right down to the roadies, soundmen and lighting crew. They've all come clean.

Two years ago, Vaughan would in all likelihood have waved a bottle of Old Crown whiskey in my face as he answered questions. At our first meeting, Stevie Ray seemed shy, inarticulate, guarded…maybe even a little frightened. He seldom volunteered more than one- or two-word answers, and rarely offered eye contact. But on this bright day in Orlando, Florida, a few hours before his show at the Bob Carr Performing Arts Centre, Stevie Ray Vaughan is a different man. He speaks with urgency and conviction, and when he makes a point, he stares me down with an intense gaze, as if to make sure I absolutely catch his drift.

The new SRV is focused, physically together and spiritually anchored. He's learned about things like humanity, commitment and responsibility. He's got the proverbial new lease on life, and is glad to be sharing the lessons he learned on the road back to sobriety. In concert nowadays, as he performs the anthemic ballad "Life without You" (a soulful, "Dock of the Bay"-type set-closer), he cautions his young audiences against getting caught up in bad habits and making the kind of mistakes he did.

On the 1986 *Live Alive* album, he used this same song to lecture about the evils of apartheid in South Africa. Now, after having experienced the humiliation of falling drunkenly from a concert stage, succumbing to a total physical collapse and finally entering a Georgia treatment facility in October of 1986, he has transformed "Life without You" into an anthem against the evils of drugs and alcohol.

In the fervor of his rap, Vaughan takes on the aura of an evangelist preacher working a crowd. But this is no hollow pitch; Stevie Ray means every word he says, from the bottom of his heart—from the bottom of his pain. He had, in fact, hit rock-bottom, and is now rededicating his life to his music and his friends, and to appreciating each new day as it comes. Every day that passes without a drink or a snort is another victory for Stevie Ray Vaughan. So far, he's winning big.

"I can honestly say that I'm really glad to be alive today," he begins with that dead-serious gaze. "Because left to my own devices, I would've slowly killed myself."

He takes a sip of coffee, and continues contemplatively: "I'm just doing the best I can now to keep this going...trying to grow up and remain young at the same time. I got a lot of paradoxes in my life. I guess I'm a real confused person. But there are some focused parts to my life now, and I'm slowly trying to put all the pieces back together."

One important part of his therapy is hard work. For the past

18 months, Stevie Ray has been touring relentlessly. Backed by Double Trouble (drummer Chris Layton, bassist Tommy Shannon and keyboardist Reese Wynans), he opened the first leg of Robert Plant's North American tour, before flying to Europe to headline summer blues festivals in Italy, Germany, Belgium and Holland. He's been so booked solid with one-nighters that he probably won't get into a studio to begin working on his next album until August—perhaps not even until September.

Meanwhile, touring is good for him. And now that he's a picture of physical fitness (he and the crew now spend free time on the road working out with weights and playing hoops—instead of imbibing), he's performing with a vitality that just wasn't there before.

"It had gotten to the point where—you know, you can't give somebody a dollar if you ain't got one. You can try all you want, but if you're out of gas, you just cannot give anymore. This was around the time we were mixing the *Live Alive* album. It was a real crazy period for all of us—for a long time we had a schedule that was just completely out of hand. And the only reason we put up with it was because, partly from the situation we were in and partly from doing too much coke, we thought we were superhuman. I mean, the whole deal is that, when you walk on stage, you're up there bigger than life. People idolize you. And if you let that go to your head, you're in trouble. You have to keep those things in perspective, but that's hard to do when you're high on cocaine and drinking all the time."

Stevie Ray sighs. "We began to see that this schedule was taking its toll. During that period we were touring and making a record. My trick was not to sleep at all. I would stay in the studio all night long, doing mixes of the live stuff and choosing tunes. I'd leave the studio about noon, go to the hotel to grab a shower, go to the sound check and play the gig. Then I'd come back to the studio, stay there all night doing mixes, come back to the hotel the next noon, grab a shower, go to the sound check and play the gig. Then I'd come back to the studio. And then the whole thing would start all over again."

He shakes his head in disbelief. "For two straight weeks I did that. We had spread ourselves way too thin, tried to put our fingers in too many parts of the pie at the same time. It was taking its toll, and the only way we could see to deal with that was, 'Oh, you're too tired? Well, here, snort some of this.'

"And between the coke and the alcohol, it had gotten to the point where I no longer had any idea what it would take to get drunk. I passed the stage where I could drink whatever I wanted to and be able to hold my liquor, so to speak. One day I could drink a quart, and then the next day all I'd have to do was drink one sip to get completely smashed."

He doesn't remember exactly how much he drank the night he fell off the stage in London. Two, maybe three drinks. Maybe a quart. But it was painfully obvious at that point that something had gone dreadfully haywire with the reigning star of the rock and blues scene. John Hammond's promising protégé was drowning in a morass of self-destruction.

"I would wake up and guzzle something, just to get rid of the pain I was feeling. Whiskey, beer, vodka, whatever was handy. It got to the point where if I'd try to say 'hi' to somebody, I would just fall apart, crying and everything. It was like...solid doom. There really was nowhere to go but up. I'd been trying to pull myself up by my bootstraps, so to speak, but they were broken, you know?"

He exacerbated his mental, physical and spiritual decline with the help of some unfortunate "recreational" activities, the most effective of which involved pouring cocaine into his drinks to prolong the buzz. "I tore up my stomach real bad by doing that. I didn't realize that the cocaine would crystallize in my stomach and make cuts inside there. Finally, I had a breakdown. I mean, everything fell apart. I surrendered to the fact that I didn't know how to go without the stuff. I had envisioned myself just staying high for the rest of my life, you know? But I had to give up to win, because I was in a losing battle."

In September of 1986, he entered a clinic in London, under the care and supervision of Dr. Victor Bloom. "He filled me in on the disease of alcoholism, and made me realize that this thing had been going on for a long time with me, long before I ever started playing professionally. Fact is, I had been drinking since 1960—when I was six years old. That's when I first started stealing Daddy's drinks. When my parents were gone, I'd find the bottle and make myself one. I thought it was cool...thought the kids down the street would think it was cool. That's where it began, and I had been depending on it ever since."

Stevie Ray readily admits that just prior to his breakdown, the constant intake and build-up of drugs and alcohol in his system contributed to a decline in the quality of his playing, and in his band's overall performance.

"Sure, it affected my playing. Of course, my thinking was, 'Boy, don't that sound good?' And there were some great notes that came out, but not necessarily always by my doing. It was kind of like I was getting carried through something. I just wasn't in control; nobody was. We were all exhausted. You could hear it on the tapes of the stuff we had to pull from for the *Live Alive* album. Some of those European gigs were okay; some of them sounded like they were the work of half-dead people.

How, Stevie Ray is asked, was he able to continue as a working artist under such terrible circumstances?

"Part of the deal," he replies, "was that this kind of behavior is so accepted in this industry. It's a classic line: 'Golly, he sure is screwed up, but he sure can play good.' "

Like so many others, Stevie Ray found there were fringe benefits to living the "high" life:

"I found out that if I stayed loaded all the time, my ego got patted on the back, and I didn't have to worry about things that I should've been thinking about. It was a lot more comfortable to run from responsibilities. There were a lot of things I was running from, and one of them was me. I was a 33-year-old with a six-year-old kid inside of me, scared and wondering where love is."

Charlie Parker, Jimi Hendrix, Jaco Pastorius—all were musical geniuses who drowned their fears and sorrows and anger in drugs and drink. Stevie Ray came perilously close to sharing their terrible fate. "But I didn't have the nuts to do it all the way," he confesses.

"And I had a lot of help and support from people, so I was able to see my problem. I came to realize that the alcohol problem, the drug problem and the fear were all symptoms of an underlying problem that's called 'lack of love.' Once you really become an addict or an alcoholic, the drink and drugs just take the place of people you care about, and of those people who care about you. You forget how to love—you reject love. You become consumed by fear.

"I was walking around trying to act cool, like I had no fear at all. But I was afraid—afraid that somebody would find out just how scared I was.

"Now I'm finally realizing that fear is the opposite of love."

These days, when Stevie Ray sings "Ain't Gone 'n' Give up on Love" in concert, the song holds a new, deeper meaning for him. And when he comes to the verse "Love's not gonna give up on me," he's quick to add: "or you!" Having seen the light, he's spreading the message, reaching out to those hordes of guitar freaks and blues lovers who have loyally followed and admired him.

"The music, to me, has become really important. All along, there have been good reasons to play—I like it, a lot of other people like it, it's fun. But beyond that, it can help us out in all kinds of ways. Music really is a way to reach out and hold on to each other in a healthy way. I'm finding that out now. It's helped me to open up more and take a chance on loving people, instead of just isolating and suspecting everybody that I run into."

A smile breaks across his somber face as he adds, "There's just a lot more reason to live now. I can't blame the music for what I got into. I had just kind of misplaced what was really going on with my life. There were a lot of mistakes made and now I can try and learn from those. It took all the crap I went through to come out on this side, and now I can try to make amends wherever I can. I've been sober now for 18 months and six days, counting today. I'm discovering that it's really a wonderful world out there; I just have to open my eyes to it."

During his month-long stay in the treatment facility, Stevie Ray was able to slow down, take stock of himself and begin building a new, healthier life. But the battle is far from over, as he explains.

"To show you how crazy this disease of alcoholism is, on the way to the treatment center I borrowed 10 dollars from my mother, telling her I was going to buy some duty-free cigarettes. Instead, I went straight to the bar and spent all the money as quick as I could on double shots of Crown, because I realized that I had never been on a plane sober before. Here I had just come out of the clinic in London, had gotten some information about what was wrong with me, learned all about what the problem was and how to deal with it, and still fell right back into that old thinking. I mean, I was on my way to go into a treatment facility, yet my first thought was, 'Wow, I've never done this straight before.' That's the type of thinking that we alcoholics have to defend against for the rest of our lives, though we take it one day at a time. Take care of today—that's the idea."

While in the Marietta treatment facility, Stevie Ray was visited by friends who'd been pulling for him all along. "I had tremendous amounts of support," he sighs. "I still do, from people in the band, the road crew, my mother, my girlfriend, other people who were in the program themselves. A lot of people wrote, called and gave support, because they had gone through things like this. Those people saved my life, and now every day that I live, it never fails—somewhere along the line, in the course of a day, I get reminded about those people."

Jackson Browne is one of those people. He first met Stevie Ray in 1982, at the Montreaux Festival in Switzerland, before the Texas blues man had a record deal. Stevie Ray's blues prowess so impressed Browne that he invited him and his band to use his home studio at no cost. The two remained friendly through the success of *Texas Flood* ('83), *Couldn't Stand the Weather* ('84), *Soul to Soul* ('85) and *Live Alive* ('86). And when Stevie Ray finally crashed, his old pal Jackson was there with a helping hand.

Another visitor to the treatment facility was Eric Clapton, himself no stranger to the evils of self-abuse. Clapton had tried counseling Stevie Ray about his drinking problem years earlier, but as Vaughan recalls, "Back then he could sense that I wasn't ready, so he didn't push it. See, you can try, you can let somebody know what's going on, but if they're not ready, you can't make 'em quit. They're gonna despise you for it and resent the fact that you tried to tell them how to live their life. People in that situation get defensive, they try to act tough and convince themselves, 'Oh, they don't know what they're missing.' And they die inside that way. They really want to say, 'I need help,' but don't know how anymore."

Clapton met Stevie Ray a few years ago, when both were touring Australia. "He was leaving the hotel, and I went out to talk to him, hangover and all. He was sober, of course, and was really calm the whole while I sat there downing two, three shots of Crown. And he just sort of wisely looked at me and said, 'Well, sometimes you gotta go through that, don'tcha?' If I had been ready to stop then and there, he would've gone on with the next part of it—but he understood that I wasn't. I wouldn't reach that point until I was literally falling off stages, about a couple of years later."

One man who tried to set Stevie Ray straight along the way was blues hero and father-figure Albert King.

"He's someone I've respected all my life, somebody I've looked up to musically and as a person. In fact, there were several times when he said he was like my daddy. He tried to talk to me on several occasions, but I never listened. Why? Because I was hooked, man. I had to learn for myself. I had to reach the bottom before I could see clearly.

"One time in particular," he says of Albert, "we were doing a show together, and he walked in backstage and said, 'We gonna have a heart-to-heart. I been watching you wrestle with that bottle three, four times already. I tell you what, man: I like to drink a little bit when I'm at home. But the gig ain't no time to get high.'

"He was trying to tell me to take care of business, to give myself a break, but I did my usual deal of trying to act like I had it all together, you know? 'Hey, ain't nuthin' wrong, man. I'm leading the life,' and all that bullshit. I was trying not to see it, but I realize now that it's like this: I don't drink or get high because I have all these problems; I have all these problems because I drink and get high. I realize now that nothing's so bad that getting drunk or getting high is gonna make it any better. Period."

He laughs aloud and adds, "Man, sobering up really screws up your drinking. And for that I'm real grateful."

Stevie Ray, a white plume in his black Zorro hat fluttering behind him, plays "Pride and Joy" and does the stroll across the huge stage of Fort Lauderdale's Sunrise Music Theater. It's a little crowd-pleasing trick he may have picked up from fellow-Texan Albert Collins. He beams as he comps on his beat-up old '59 Strat, raking the strings in smooth, circular motions to accentuate the shuffle groove. On the slow blues of "Texas Flood," he digs for roots, dipping deeply into the Albert King bag, just as Jimi Hendrix did on "Red House" and a host of other tunes.

On Howlin' Wolf's "Tell Me," Stevie Ray reaches for some of the raunch of Hubert Sumlin—or Lowell Fulson or Jimmy Rogers. And on "Mary Had a Little Lamb," he pulls out the smooth, fleet-fingered licks that made Buddy Guy a guitar hero. He pays tribute to Freddy King with the classic instrumental "Hideaway," before launching into his own hard-rocking "Scuttle Buttin'," stretching each tune to 10 searing minutes or more.

Stevie Ray is a bit hoarse this night, so he tries to preserve his voice as much as possible. Backstage before the show, he had a certified massage therapist work him over with a little shiatsu on the back of the neck, to loosen up those tight muscles and alleviate strain on the voice box. "I've got an acupuncturist who does wonders for me," he says, "but he's back in New York. He won't travel, so I gotta do what I can on the road."

After a rousing shuffle blues version of the Beatles' "Taxman," Stevie Ray introduces special guest Otis Rush. The Chicago bluesman, another boyhood hero of Vaughan's, steps onto the Sunrise stage toting his trusty righty Gibson Stereo 345 (which he flips over and plays lefty, à la Albert King and Jimi Hendrix). The two guitarists have not rehearsed together, and Rush barely had time for a sound check. He's playing through a Marshall stack, and his semi-hollow Gibson feeds back terribly through the first couple of songs, until the soundmen finally zero in on the proper eq adjustments.

Stevie and Otis jump into a mid-tempo shuffle. Otis is warming up now, and the crowd is clearly warming up to him. By the time he lays into "Stormy Monday," he has this auditorium of young blues fans in the palm of his hand. Many in the crowd have probably never heard of him before, but after a blazing rendition of "Got My Mojo Working," they're well-acquainted with the man. Some will no doubt follow up this first encounter with a trip to the record store, and head straight for the blues bins.

And for this, Stevie Ray Vaughan deserves all the credit in the world. He is the premier figure in today's blues world; his drawing power at the box office is even greater than that of B.B. King. But Stevie Ray reveres his blues fathers—B.B., Albert, Freddy and Earl King, Albert Collins, Otis Rush, Buddy Guy, Hubert Sumlin, Jimmy Rogers—the list goes on and on. And, whenever possible, he goes out of his way to repay his debt to them. The wild cheering for Otis Rush at the Sunrise Music Theater reflects—and is the outgrowth of—Stevie Ray's gratitude.

It is boundless. At this year's New Orleans Jazz Heritage Festival, Stevie Ray brought out special guest Albert Collins, and the two exchanged licks well into the night. At the Chicago Blues Festival a couple of years back, he mixed it up on stage with the great Buddy Guy. And down around his home stomping grounds, the Austin-Dallas-Fort Worth network, he regularly goes toe-to-toe with the local celebrity six-stringers.

It's all a matter of personal and musical responsibility, says Stevie Ray. "Those guys are the ones who really ought to have the recognition," he maintains. "They're the pioneers and the innovators, and they deserve respect for that. All the great records by Albert King and Albert Collins, Otis Rush, B.B. King's *Live at the Regal*—there's millions we could talk about, and each one of them is unbelievable in its own right. They're like books, in a sense. You can reread them and gain a new insight each time. They never sound the same—not to me anyway. There's always something new to learn in each one. So these great blues men, they've all been like my teachers.

"I think I've got something special to say with my music. But I have to keep these things in perspective, because they're gifts. It's all a gift, and I have to keep giving it back or it goes away. If I start believing that it's all my doing, it's gonna be my undoing. And I'm committing myself to doing the most I can with the gifts I have, so that they do as many people as much good as possible."

Stevie Ray has stopped running from himself. He's been through some rough times, and now he's all the stronger for it—physically, mentally, spiritually and musically. You can hear it in his voice when he sings. You can hear it in his solos. All the crutches have been removed, leaving…the new and improved Stevie Ray Vaughan.

"And now I realize that it's my responsibility to stay sober, and to reach out to anybody who's got a problem with it. If I'm in a position to give any kind of help to them and don't, then what have I done? Hell, if it hadn't been for people reaching out to me, I may not have made it."

He pauses, sets his last cup of coffee on the table and points to a small, white lapel pin bearing the familiar, frizzy-haired visage of Jimi Hendrix.

"You know," he begins urgently, "there's a big lie in this business—that it's okay to go out in flames. But that really doesn't do anybody much good. I may be wrong, but I think Hendrix was trying to come around. I think he had gotten a glimpse of what he needed to change and that he really wanted to change. And I found myself in a similar position."

His voice drops to a solemn whisper as he adds, "Some people can be examples about going ahead and growing. And some people, unfortunately, don't make it there, and end up being examples because they had to die. I hit rock bottom, but thank God my bottom wasn't death."

GUITAR WORLD, JUNE 1989

STEP BY STEP

A sober SRV discusses his new album, IN STEP.
By Andy Aledort

THE STEVIE RAY Vaughan of this interview, which took place just before the release of *In Step*, was markedly different from the SRV of old. Sobriety had put him more in touch with his innermost feelings, brought him face to face with his greatest fears and weaknesses. Kicking drugs and alcohol had given him the opportunity to have, in his words, a "new life." This was a more serious Stevie Ray, one intent on using the media to transmit the lessons he'd learned to anyone who would listen, and, more important, those who most needed to.

All the seriousness did not, however, drown out the vibrant enthusiasm that had always been so much a part of his character. Now he greeted people with bear hugs strong enough to crush a Sequoia tree. And when he spoke, he looked right into your eyes. Stevie had become a man determined not to waste any opportunity to communicate.

GUITAR WORLD: How long has it been since you recorded the last studio album, *Soul to Soul*?
STEVIE RAY VAUGHAN: Four years. We cut *Soul to Soul* in May of '85.
GW: Why has it taken four years to record another studio album?

VAUGHAN: I guess the world had to turn around a few times, and so did I.

GW: How has playing music changed for you since you came out of drug rehabilitation?

VAUGHAN: I thought the hardest thing would be, "Oh God, now I'm straight—can I still play?" But that had nothing to do with it. The hardest part is trying to keep things in perspective. I found out that the biggest problem that I had was self-centeredness and ego. That's really what my addiction seems to boil down to. [*chuckles*] To keep that part of myself under control while everybody's telling you how great you are is quite a task.

GW: It must be very difficult to see what's really going on without being swayed by what people tell you.

VAUGHAN: Yeah. Finding some kind of perspective is the hardest part, because I want to stay alive and I want to stay as healthy as possible, and grow in that way. And while it's getting a lot easier in some ways, every time I think I've learned something, I realize that I've just uncovered a big hole! [*laughs*] A big empty spot, or one that's going, "ARGHHH!"

GW: Being a blues musician is about expressing your feelings, and communicating them to the audience. How has the emotional upheaval you've experienced affected you as a musician?

VAUGHAN: One thing I've noticed is that songs I used to sing at people, I should have been singing at myself. At least I think that way.

GW: Do you hear the words more now?

VAUGHAN: Oh God, yeah. Songs mean different things than I used to think they did, too. To put it mildly, a lot of blues tunes have to do with resentments, big time. [*laughs*] Take "Cold Shot." I used to sing that at certain women that I've been involved with over the years. Even though I didn't write it, I had in my head the way I related to it. Since I sobered up, I realized that I left; I was the one who gave the cold shot. And it hurts when you realize that you've hurt somebody, as opposed to, all this time, you've been telling yourself how bad they hurt you. A lot of times, if I stop and look at it, those words could really be telling me that I hurt myself. There are also other songs that are kinder than I thought. They make me feel better than I knew.

GW: What are you finding there that makes it feel so good?

VAUGHAN: A whole new world. A whole new chance for myself. More so than ever, if I don't play the best that I possibly can, and really try to play better than I think I can, then I've wasted it. Because I'm playing on borrowed time. Left to my own devices, I would have killed myself, however slowly or whatever. Now I have a new chance. My best thinking just about killed me, okay? It just so happens that I'm not dead! [*laughs*] Somebody else helped me to stay alive—I just allowed it to happen.

GW: How did you manage to capture those feelings on the new record?

VAUGHAN: Most of the time, the whole band played together live. It was kind of a difficult record to make. We had fun, but we started and stopped a lot because I was having amp problems.

GW: What happened to the amps you used on *Soul to Soul*?

VAUGHAN: They weren't holding up. I'd turn 'em on, set them to a real good sound, turn them off to let them cool down, and when it was time to play and I'd turn 'em back on, one of them would die. They would either start going, "ACKHHKHK" or "BLLPPPP" or blow up. [*laughs*] I'd hit a couple of notes and it would start making horrible noises. The setup changed from day to day. The amps were dying like flies. This sounds crazy, but I took 32 amps with me. If worse comes to worse, I thought, there'll always be something I can pull out of a road case. I'm glad I took so many amps, because we ended up having only about three or four that worked. In fact, I ended up buying an old '59 Fender Bassman that ended up being my main amp for the whole album. I loved it! It was the one amp that stayed right the whole time. All these new-fangled custom amps I had kept falling apart.

But perhaps the weirdest part of recording this album was that I had to stand in this thing that looked like a square baseball backstop, made out of chicken wire, while I played my parts. There was either a radio station or some kind of microwave stuff that came through the studio—you'd be playing along, and all of a sudden there'd be these weird clicks and buzzes coming out of the amps—but if I stood inside this cage that they made, it wouldn't happen. They caged me! [*laughs*]

GW: What other amps did you end up using?

VAUGHAN: Usually, I had one Dumble, one Marshall, the Bassman and a Super Reverb. I ran them all at the same time, but they were miked differently and set differently. Sometimes, I ran the effects through them—when I say effects, I'm not talking about space stations, I'm talking about a Fuzz Face, a Tube Screamer or a wah-wah pedal. I also had a Leslie in another room.

GW: Stevie Wonder is an example of an artist who has been able to write great music that also carries a message, which is a hard thing to do. I think you've done it very successfully with the songs on this record; the last thing you'd want to do is to sound "preachy."

VAUGHAN: No, I really don't want that. It seems real important to me to write about that stuff. I spent so long with this…[*lets out a long, slow exhale*]…image of, "I'm cooler than so-and-so because I get higher than he does." And I really believed it for a long time. But it's just not true.

GW: Life doesn't have to be an "Iron Man" contest.

VAUGHAN: No, it doesn't! [*laughs*] And I'd just as soon spend the rest of these years making it clear that it's not true.

GW: Was it hard to get these feelings down in a song?

VAUGHAN: I went back and forth between feeling really strongly about it and wondering if anybody really wants to hear this shit or not. I knew that I meant it, that I felt good about it sometimes. I was afraid that I'd turn people off. Somewhere along the line that stopped mattering because, with what I was trying to say, if they got turned off, it'd only be for a temporary time. I've been there before, when somebody would try to tell me that I had a problem. I'd go [*in a growl*], "Of course I do! God damn it, don't you think I know that?" I just had to come to grips with it.

GW: How did you develop your soloing style?

VAUGHAN: It's a real weird mixture. It's kind of everything from my generation to Muddy Waters at the same time. It goes back to my brother Jimmie, when he was bringing home all these different records. Maybe it was because I was a little kid, but it seemed like he brought home the Bluesbreakers with Eric Clapton, Howlin' Wolf, B.B. King, Muddy Waters and the Beatles—all at the same time. It was like, "Here comes Jimmie with the record world!" [*laughs*]

GW: The whole history of recorded music was under his arm!

VAUGHAN: Yeah! And he knew what he was doing. At the same time, the son of some friends of my parents would come over with his guitar, and he'd show us Jimmy Reed stuff. Here's all this going on, and then somewhere real soon down the line, Jimmie brings home this Jimi Hendrix record, and we both went, "AHHHH! What's this?!"

GW: Was it *Are You Experienced?*

VAUGHAN: That, and a 45, I think. All at the same time, there were all these different influences. By the time I was 12, Jimmie was gone. Here he was, the hottest guitar player I knew of, and was considered the hottest guitar player in Texas at age 15. I think he started playing when he was 12. [*laughs*]

GW: Wasn't he called "Freddie King, Jr." when he was 15?

VAUGHAN: Yeah, he was. I mean, what do you do but get excited when all this is going on? If you want to know what made me go crazy with it, it was watching Jimmie. Not trying to outdo him, but, shit, what do you do but pick up the ball and run? It wasn't trying to pass him, and it wasn't trying to keep up with him. It was more like, "Wow! Look what big brother stumbled onto!" A lot of people seem to think that we're trying to beat each other at something, but it's not that at all. I saw him get real exciting—not just excited, but exciting—with something, and that excited me. I didn't know what else to do!

GW: What were some of the slow blues you heard that helped you develop your style?

VAUGHAN: Albert King records, for one thing. B.B. King's *Live at the Regal* (MCA, 1971), Albert King's *Born under a Bad Sign* (Atlantic, 1967), it was called first, or *King of the Blues Guitar.* Believe it or not, I remember seeing Albert King on TV, doing "Born under a Bad

Sign," and I was like, "YES!!!"

GW: What is it about the blues that makes it so vital and powerful?

VAUGHAN: It just sounds more like "the real thing" than anything else. Like I said, it's not [*in a dry, monotone*], "This is cooler than this," or "This has more emotion." When I heard the blues, it killed me, it slayed me! There was just no question. I heard it all these different ways, from the English blues boom to authorized recordings to shitty bootleg stuff of everybody you can dream of. It's funny, because I don't like that there are bootlegs of me out there, but I'm glad I got to hear everyone else's!

GW: Have your feelings for the blues changed over the years?

VAUGHAN: In recent years, I feel like I've gotten more in touch with it. It's usually when I go and see somebody play who's used to playing clubs, and isn't used to running around in a fancy tour bus and playing arenas.

GW: Can you hear that quality in your own playing when you listen back to the tape?

VAUGHAN: Sometimes, and it makes me feel good—because I know that I'm still alive.

GW: The solo on "Wall of Denial" is one of your best; you don't hold back at all.

VAUGHAN: I was jumping up and down! It was real important to us. We had fun on that, man. We had trouble with this and that on the record, but we had fun, too. I learn tricks every once in a while—ways to do things. For that solo I used a Leslie, but it was noisy on the slow speed. So I took a VARIAC, put it on the slow speed, and then put the Leslie on the fast speed, making the Leslie go a little faster than slow, without making any clunking noises as it went around.

GW: Did you use your "Number One" guitar for most of *In Step*?

VAUGHAN: No, just some of it. I used the white Strat body with a Telecaster neck on some of it. I used the butterscotch one, which is a '61. On "Wall of Denial," I used "Number One."

GW: That guitar has such a unique sound; it's like a growl.

VAUGHAN: I know! But I can't use it all the time because, for some reason, the low E wants to rattle real bad. I had to change the neck;

I took the neck off the butterscotch one and put it on "Number One." I still have the original neck. For years, Rene [*Martinez, Stevie's guitar tech*] had been taking the frets out, filling the fret slots in and then putting new frets in. Over time, the slots got too big; it's mainly on the edges. I've been using big frets for so long, it only made it worse.

The original neck has also been broken up by the headstock, which doesn't help. Have you ever seen Jimmie throw his guitar? I learned this trick from him, except his guitar never broke! [*laughs*] I was playing in Lubbock back in '81, and when I threw it, it hit this paneled wall, catching it up by the headstock, snapping the wood. It laid there on the ground, and some of the strings went up, and some of them went down! It was doing all this, "BLUBGBBNGBG!" by itself, and I was standing there, going, "Yeah!" [*laughs*] It happened during "Third Stone from the Sun," and it sounded fine, like it was supposed to be there! But I cried later.

GUITAR WORLD, JULY 1989

MORE IN STEP

Stevie Ray Vaughan weighs in on the recording of IN STEP.

By Andy Aledort

THIS INTERVIEW TOOK place on the phone, with Stevie calling from his home in Texas. We continued to speak in depth about the recording of *In Step*, and Stevie enlivened the conversation by playing musical examples through the same '59 Bassman amp he used on the album.

GUITAR WORLD: I understand that most of the basics for *In Step* were cut live. Is that how the band achieved such great interplay?

STEVIE RAY VAUGHAN: Yeah. We were able to watch each other pretty closely. We were set up so that we could play live: Tommy had an iso [*isolation*] booth for his amp, but he was in the same room with Chris; Reese [*Wynans, keyboardist*] had an iso booth for his Leslie, and I had an iso booth for me and my rig. That way I could get some response out of my rig, but I had a window so I could see in the control room on one side of the room and see Chris on the other side of the room. And we'd watch each other. Also, I had a talkback mic, so I could holler, whistle or, if I could remember the words, sing the vocal part. [*laughs*]

GW: Was everyone wearing headphones?

VAUGHAN: Yeah. We tried to record without headphones, but the main problem is that I play loud.

GW: How loud do you play in the studio as compared to a gig?

VAUGHAN: Pretty much the same. In some cases quieter, and in some cases louder. Every room sounds different. I'm trying to learn some things about wood, and the characteristics of the sound. Kiva Studios, where we recorded the album, is a completely wooden room—finished wood—and if I wasn't real careful, I would've ended up having a sound that was too dark. In the studio, my Bassman was set so it sounded so crystalline, so clear and high-endy, but when I got it home, it sounded horrible!

Back to what we were talking about: As a rule, this way seemed to be an easier way to record. For one thing, we all had our own separate mix. We each had a little mixing board right next to us so we could make our own headphone mixes. We were all able to watch each other, and that way we were playing to each other and with each other, cueing off each other, so that it was real spontaneous. At the same time, there was good separation because of the iso booths, and the drums were in the big room to get the big sound. And Tommy was in there, too, feeling it with Chris. It worked out real well.

When we did *Soul to Soul*, we had every amp that I owned at the time hooked up. And they were all in the room with us! We also had a huge P.A. in there—it was some ungodly number of watts—with a 30-inch sub-woofer, which we used for monitors! [*laughs*] For amps, I had two Dumbles, a couple of Marshalls, a bunch of Fenders, and then it trailed off to the side. It was kind of like a galaxy of amps—it spread out like the Milky Way! We just had some foam rubber between my amps and the drums.

GW: Did that result in the loss of some realistic separation?

VAUGHAN: Yeah, it did. We had to go in and dissect things, and take some of the "bleed" out. There was less "bleed" than we thought there would be, but you can hear some ghost vocals on that record. The isolation we used for *In Step* worked better, and I was still next to my rig, so I could get the response.

GW: How long did it take to record *In Step*?

VAUGHAN: Fifteen weeks, start to finish. That's not counting the writing of the songs. We had a couple of breaks to do different things.

GW: How long did *Soul to Soul* take?

VAUGHAN: About three months. That's a realistic amount of time. If we get it done faster, great, but I don't like to lock myself into six weeks, you know? Some people spend a real long time in the studio, but I wouldn't want to get stuck like that. You tend to take the songs apart, put 'em back together, and you end up sterilizing them. I've heard of people slaving together four or five 24-track machines, and you have a zillion tracks going at once. I don't see that as a solution, but I like to leave myself room so that I don't feel too pressured. At the same time I don't want to feel like I don't have to do any work because, given the space, I can be a procrastinator. I like a fixed amount of time, within reason. I like to work at a relaxed pace, but I do like to get back out on the road. We didn't have too much of a chance to get out on the road with the songs on this record, until the end.

GW: How many extra tunes were there?

VAUGHAN: There were five more that we recorded, with two versions of one of them.

GW: Were any of these Hendrix tunes?

VAUGHAN: No, not this time. There are several that I'm in love with, like "Stepping Stone" and, of course, "The Wind Cries Mary," "Angel" and "Freedom."

GW: Once you get going, it's hard to stop.

VAUGHAN: Sure is! [*laughs*] I don't know all of them, though. Some of 'em, I know mostly how it goes, which is okay, because it ends up not being just a copy. There are a lot that we'd like to record, but it was important to us that this record shows were we come from, as much as possible. In fact, I was afraid there wasn't enough blues on it. As it turns out, we actually recorded a few more blues tunes that didn't make the record. We recorded "Boot Hill" [*released posthumously on* The Sky Is Crying], and I play slide on the whole thing. It's a Sly Williams song.

I used my Charlie Christian guitar for that, and it sounded horrible—the right kind of horrible. [*laughs*] It was real fat. It sounded like it's supposed to. But, once again, we keep trying to do it in a key that's too high for me to sing. And I should know by now, because we've recorded that song for every record except *Texas Flood*. And we did it too high again! The track does sound real good, though. We'll do it again, in a lower key next time. I've got my Charlie Christian with me on the road now, tuned down to C# or C, I forget which one.

GW: Is that the key you can sing it in?

VAUGHAN: Yeah.

GW: "Crossfire" reminds me of some of the Albert King stuff that was recorded at Stax.

VAUGHAN: Yeah. The first time I heard that song, it reminded me of Junior Walker a whole lot. I thought it was a neat song, but it was arranged in a slightly different way, and I was uncomfortable playing it. I didn't know what to play! And it was hard to admit that I didn't know what to play. I just said, "This is weird!" [*laughs*]

GW: It was the song's fault.

VAUGHAN: Yeah. "This song's weird, man!" But then I came to grips with it. I had to let the band carry the riff, and it has taken me a while to learn to let the band carry what they're going to carry anyway, you know? I don't have to be all over everything to make it work.

But there are songs that never get finished. I think of them as babies that never grow up. It's funny, because I went through a grieving process when we were done tracking. I felt bad for the songs that were never completely recorded, so I just sat in my room and played them by myself. I played my babies that never grew up.

GW: Did you record anything on the National steel guitar that you're holding in the cover photo?

VAUGHAN: Not this time, but I had planned on it. I did record one song, "Life by the Drop," by myself with the 12-string acoustic. I recorded it that way because it sounded more personal. However, the more we worked on it—I did several takes—the more the producer and myself heard it as a band song. I may go in and record it with the guy who wrote it, Doyle Bramhall—the father, not the son.

GW: In "Tightrope," there is the lyric, "There was love all around me, but I was looking for revenge. Thank God it never found me, would have been the end." What's that about?

VAUGHAN: A lot of times, our fears keep us from seeing what's really there. I realized the other day when I got a glimpse of what life would be like without my fears, without my guilt and my shame—without that club to beat myself over the head with. It was just for a couple of minutes, and I realized that without that stuff... I never realized how much those feelings and those emotions permeate everything. I got a glimpse of how I felt without all of that, and I felt a lot better about everything and everybody. It was a real neat deal. I was just talking to somebody, and they said something that sparked it. It was like being in a completely smoke-filled room—like a cloud—and then somebody turned on a vent and all the smoke was gone for a minute.

I learned all that stuff—the guilt and the shame—when I was a little kid; I learned how to be afraid all the time because it wasn't very "constant" at home. I don't know if everybody else in the family perceived it the same way; probably not. But I learned real quickly not to know what to expect, so therefore I'd just stay out of the way, keep my feelings out of the way. If I did have feelings, it must have been my fault, because that's what I heard when the fights were going on. I didn't realize how deeply that was embedded in me. Without someone else doing it, I do it to myself, because I'm familiar with that, you know? It's a shame.

GW: For whatever the reason, that stuff is self-sustaining.

VAUGHAN: Uh-huh. I'm just now learning how to let go of some of that, and I can't always do it. Sometimes, I can put the club down. And other times, I pick it right back up and go to flogging myself! [*laughs*] It's an old pattern that I have to learn how to not do.

GW: Do those feelings ever come out while you're playing?

VAUGHAN: Sometimes they crawl all over me. It happened the other night: We were playing along, and all of a sudden I start feeling all of this self-conscious crap crawling all over me. You just want to tear your skin off and run!

GW: It's like a vine crawling up your leg.

VAUGHAN: Yeah, except, believe me, it's already all over my head! [*laughs*] And then I opened my eyes and saw all these people watching us, really having a blast, and I thought, "What am I doing to myself? These people accept us. I'm the only one who's not accepting myself right now." There's something to always wanting to be better; it gives us a reason to try to grow. But it's not all right to allow myself to be unaccepting of everything. The audience was honestly enjoying what we were doing, and I was sabotaging it! It's an easy thing to do, sometimes. But, in reality, all I have to do is stop and look where I've come from. That has to do with how my life is changing for the better. If I stop and look at where I found myself before I got clean... Where I'm at now is a little better than when I was puking up blood and bile in the middle of the street, and then getting up and going, "Hey man, I think I need a drink."

GW: When I saw you at the Pier in New York last summer, there was this relentless intensity to your guitar playing that was just incredible. I had wondered how your problems with drug addiction would affect your playing. What I heard was a tremendous outpouring of good feelings.

VAUGHAN: Well, I have to keep trying. And I do. I know that everything is better now, and I do mean everything. My whole life is better. It's hard for me to see that when everything is better, that includes the music, too. There's no reason why it shouldn't. I'm not saying that it's an automatic deal—I have to work at these things harder than ever. And that's fine with me. I'm glad I do. It has to do with progression, and there's healthy and unhealthy sides to it. The balance is the thing to try to find.

GW: Do the slide-ups at the beginning of your version of "Love Me Darlin' " come from Hubert Sumlin's playing on the original?

VAUGHAN: Yeah. It's just more evident because I've got my Fuzz Face on, and I get more of a ripping sound. Hubert had a real crystal-clear sound, almost too crystal clear to be true. I've always tried to figure out how in the hell he got that sound. I still haven't gotten it! I've gotten close, but he gets this natural sound.

GW: How did the song "Travis Walk" come about?

VAUGHAN: We were in a rehearsal hall, working on "Scratch 'n' Sniff," and we couldn't decide what we wanted to do. We stopped for a minute; everybody was real frustrated. I walked over to the corner, looked at this picture of my brother, and jumped into playing the tune! [*laughs*] He just looked so cool in the picture.

GW: When you write, do you think at all about the style the tunes are in, or where they're coming from?

VAUGHAN: It's just a sound I hear in my head, and a feeling I have. I don't know how to decipher between my thoughts and my feelings, and, in a way, that's real good. It's confusing sometimes, when you're trying to weed through 'em, but when I hear something, it makes me feel a certain way. And when I feel something, often I'll hear certain things. Then, I try to act on it in a constructive way, which is to play.

GW: On this record, you've brought in some different grooves and different feelings that you haven't in the past, on such songs as "Tightrope," "Crossfire" and "Wall of Denial."

VAUGHAN: I keep trying to make it all come out. I can't read or write music, so sometimes, in trying to find things, I just stick my hand on the neck. Sometimes it's a surprise, and sometimes it becomes what I wanted to hear. I visualize things—sometimes I visualize correctly, sometimes I don't. As a result, some of my favorite things to play started as mistakes!

GW: Speaking of mistakes: I've heard that the live album [*Live Alive*] is something that you're not very happy with.

VAUGHAN: Well, God, I wasn't in very good shape. I didn't realize how bad a shape I was in at the time. There were more fix-it jobs done on the album than I would have liked.

GW: I think "Texas Flood" is a shining moment on that album.

VAUGHAN: That was from the Montreaux Jazz Festival, and we felt good about what we were doing. Overall, there were some good nights and some good gigs, but it was more haphazard than we would have liked.

GW: What would you put on your "essential listening" list?

VAUGHAN: Buddy Guy's *A Man and the Blues* even though he himself doesn't like the record. [*laughs*] B.B. King's *Live at the Regal*, Grant Green's *Live at the Lighthouse*—it's not blues, but it's wonderful—anything by Donny Hathaway, especially the *Donny Hathaway: Live* album; it kills me. There's a lot of gospel stuff that I love, but not necessarily up-to-date stuff. People sometimes turn me on to things that aren't new at all.

Of course, I love a lot of Albert King, but I don't know what my favorite would be. There's all kinds of stuff! Hendrix kind of goes without saying. I like just about everything by him. Keep in mind that I go through phases with all of these people, and phases with what I listen to. It's not that I think one is more important than the other; it has to do with what I can take in. I can't take it all in at once. I haven't been home for a while, and I need to dig back into my records.

GUITAR WORLD, DECEMBER 1990

THE SKY IS CRYING

Nowhere was the loss of Stevie Ray Vaughan
more keenly felt than in the cities of Austin and Dallas.

By Bill Milkowski

MONDAY, AUGUST 27—AUSTIN

The first flash comes over the Associated Press wire at about seven a.m.: "Copter crash in East Troy, Wisconsin. Five fatalities, including a musician."

Keen-eyed staffers at the Austin *American Statesman* catch that item and begin putting two and two together. The AP updates its story every half hour with fresh details: The mysterious "musician" soon becomes "a member of Eric Clapton's entourage"—and then, "a guitarist." By 9:30, rumors spread that Stevie Ray Vaughan, Austin's favorite son, was aboard the doomed craft.

At 11:30, Clapton's manager confirms the worst: Vaughan was indeed among the passengers in the five-seat helicopter, which slammed into a fog-shrouded hillside near southeastern Wisconsin's Alpine Valley ski resort. Stevie Ray had boarded the aircraft after performing in an enormous blues show at the resort, and taken part in an all-star finale/jam on Robert Johnson's "Sweet Home Chicago." The program and the jam featured Stevie Ray, Eric Clapton, Robert Cray, Jimmie Vaughan and Chicago blues legend Buddy Guy, all of whom ripped it up before an ecstatic crowd of 25,000.

Four Bell 260B Jet Ranger helicopters awaited the artists and their respective entourages following the jam. Because of poor traffic conditions at Alpine Valley—only one two-lane road leads from the venue, and gridlock delays of an hour or more are common—major acts usually depart via helicopter.

The caravan of blues stars departed from Alpine Valley at two-minute intervals. The first, second and fourth copters landed without incident at Chicago's Meigs Field. The third, bearing members of Clapton's entourage and Stevie Ray, never made it. Poor visibility due to dense fog is prominent among factors blamed for the disaster. (The Austin *American-Statesman* later reports that Federal Aviation Administration records show that the pilot, Jeffrey William Brown, had two previous helicopter accidents.)

By noon, the capital city of Texas is in a state of deep shock. Stevie Ray's death is the most devastating blow to the Lone Star State's music community since Lubbock's Buddy Holly, along with Richie Valens and the Big Bopper, went down in an Iowa plane crash 31 years earlier. Residents who knew Stevie Ray walk about tearfully, dazed and disoriented.

"I've been calling people I haven't talked to in 15 years," says Austin singer-songwriter Natalie Zoe. "Everyone has been reaching out and trying to make connections with people who knew how important Stevie was to them. I mean…he was our homeboy."

By 5P.M., merchants have posted signs and hoisted banners proclaiming "We Love You Stevie" and "So Long Stevie" outside their stores. Even the Holiday Inn replaces the cheery "Welcome Conventioneers" adorning its marquee with a somber "SRV R.I.P." Plumbing stores, Tex-Mex restaurants, musical instrument stores, donut shops—all fly the flag of grief in this central Texas town, where Little Stevie Vaughan, the skinny kid from Oak Cliff, became Stevie Ray Vaughan, hometown hero and Austin's musical ambassador to the world.

Fans begin converging on Zilker Park, where, 10 years earlier, mourners gathered for a candlelight vigil on the night John Lennon was murdered. Now they sit side-by-side in the darkness, with 3,000 points of light flickering in a sea of sorrow. Tattooed Chicano bikers, lawyers in Brooks Brothers suits and crystal-wielding New Agers spread out on blankets and meditate in silence. Fans clutching photos of SRV construct shrines to the fallen guitar hero. Young gunslingers tote their Strats, Buddhists chant and old friends weep openly as disc jockey Jody Denberg of Austin's KLBJ radio pumps a steady stream of SRV through a makeshift P.A. The sound of Stevie Ray's stinging Strat pierces the night air and the hearts of the huddled blues fans, offering bittersweet solace to the bereaved.

"It's depressing and spiritually healing at the same time," says one SRV fan, who clutches an autographed copy of *Texas Flood* he'd received from the guitarist some years earlier.

Even as the mourners gather at Zilker Park, others instinctively head to the club Antone's, a focal point of the Austin blues scene throughout the mid Seventies and a favorite hangout of the Vaughan brothers over the years. Some fans have driven from as far as Oklahoma to be here in honor of Stevie Ray; others come on foot from their dorms on the campus of Texas University, listening to disc jockey Paul Ray's "Blue Monday" tribute on KTU as they walk. One fan fondly recalls the night in 1978 when Stevie Ray went toe-to-toe on stage at Antone's with Otis Rush, the great left-handed bluesman who wrote "Double Trouble," the tune after which SRV named his band. Another mourner describes the night he saw Little Stevie play with Albert King in 1975. A younger fan relates, in still-awed tones, his excitement over witnessing a 1987 jam that saw Stevie Ray and Jimmie joined by U2's The Edge and Bono.

Local TV stations begin converging on the club by nine p.m. Their cameras and microphones focus on SRV intimates, such as club owner Clifford Antone, a close friend to both Vaughan brothers.

"I met Stevie when I was 22 and he was 17," he sobs. "The kid could always play. I mean, he could play as good then as he does now. People like that...it's just born in 'em, you know? He was Little Stevie back then, just a kid. He'd hang out and play and make you laugh. It was a very simple thing. It had nothing to do with the record business, or TV or movies or any of that shit. Him, me, Jimmie, Denny Freeman, Doyle Bramhall...we were all just a bunch of kids, drawn together by our love for the blues, you know? And even in recent years, when I'd see him, I'd say, 'Howya doin', kid?' I mean, he was my friend, just this little guy who played guitar. The rest is the world's trip, you know?"

It is somehow appropriate that W.C. Clark is booked this night at Antone's. A black bluesman from East Austin, W.C. played with Stevie Ray and singer Lou Ann Barton in the late-Seventies band Triple Threat Review. Last year, the three were reunited for a special Austin City Limits program that celebrated W.C.'s 50th birthday.

"I'm dumbfounded," says Clark, appearing quite shaken. "He was an easygoing person, really lovable. I felt like a benefactor to him."

TUESDAY, AUGUST 28—AUSTIN

Still reeling from the news, the city tries to carry on. By now, every daily newspaper in the country has run some kind of front page item about the tragic loss. The world is stunned, but the people of Austin are crushed—still shaking their heads in disbelief, wondering aloud, "Why? Why now, after he had cleaned up and gotten his life back together?"

Old friends and colleagues show up at Antone's this night, to hug each other and help brush away the tears that won't quit. Doug Sahm, David Grissom, Paul Ray, Little David Murray, Derek O'Brien, Van Wilks, Marcia Ball and dozens of other Austin notables take the stage and play for Stevie Ray. And they recall both the lean years and the good times.

Natalie Zoe remembers Stevie Ray as the nice guy who lived across the street in a funky, shack-ratty house on Thornton Road, near the railroad tracks. "We were all young and broke back in the late Seventies," she says. "None of us on that street had any air conditioning, and it was hot eight months a year. So we did a lot of hanging out on porches, picking guitars and trying to stay cool. I was playing steady gigs then, and he used to help me haul my gear out of the house and into my car. He was always very gentlemanly, very neighborly. Just a nice, sweet guy."

Eddie Munoz, an old friend of Stevie's, who played guitar in the early-Eighties band the Plimsouls, recalls SRV's uncanny ability to communicate directly through his instrument. "Stevie was a rarity. There are very few people who have that much soul and that much power, who can command so much attention just by plugging in a guitar. I remember one time, a couple of years before he got signed, I was on tour with the Plimsouls and ran into him in New Orleans. We were hanging around the French Quarter, and we walked into this open-air club; a blues band was playing. There were only three people in the audience, and Stevie Ray had his guitar with him, so the band let him sit in. And within five minutes, man, there was a crowd of a hundred people milling around outside, staring at this guy piping out this hot stuff on guitar. It was wild, man. The guy could always draw crowds by plugging that thing in. But he didn't carry any big pretense about it. He used to say to me, 'I don't know where it came from. It just happened. My brother Jimmie showed me some stuff, and then it was like the dam broke.'

"He was a great guy and a decent human being," Munoz continues. "He was just so shy and unassuming—until you put a guitar in his hands. He lived for playing that guitar. Everybody's jaw dropped whenever he played. There are those people who are just so blessed—one person out of millions who can touch the instrument and have it sing for him. He always had that."

Guitarist Van Wilks remembers SRV as someone who commanded respect from all the various musical cliques around Austin. "You had all these factions here in the early Eighties—the Antone's straight blues scene, the country scene, the New Wave college scene, the younger hard rock and heavy metal scene. But Stevie was able to transcend all of that, and without even being aware of it. He was...'

Wilks becomes aware of his use of the past tense, and freezes in mid-sentence. He hangs his head, and in a hushed tone, as if the life had just run out of him, says, "Man, it just now hit me."

WEDNESDAY, AUGUST 29—AUSTIN

A young man with shoulder-length blond hair slowly guides his wheelchair through the Austin airport terminal. He wears a Stevie Ray Vaughan T-shirt and a baseball cap sporting the striking David Coleman-designed SRV logo that adorns the *In Step* album cover. He looks confused and disoriented, lost in a sea of bustling Texas businessmen. He notices my long hair, and accurately sizing me up as a brother in SRV, wheels over to talk. Without any preamble he asks, "Hey, man, where's the funeral?" He's Doug Castor, a 33-year-old fan who has made the pilgrimage to Austin from Pittsburgh. Like other fans from around the country, he wrongly assumed that Stevie Ray was born here. In a musical sense, of course, Stevie Ray was born in Austin, and the town certainly adopted him. But I inform him that the funeral will be held Friday, at noon—in Dallas.

"Dallas?! Shit! How'm I gonna get to Dallas?!" With that, he spins his chair 180 degrees and wheels over to the Avis desk, where he inquires about handicapped-equipped rental cars. "I really can't afford this," he tells me, "but I just gotta be there. His music touched me in an important way."

That night at The Steamboat, another Austin guitar hero, Eric Johnson, dedicates his set to Stevie Ray. It is another cathartic act in a town coming to grips with cold, harsh reality.

THURSDAY, AUGUST 30–DALLAS

En route to a candlelight vigil in Oak Cliff, I tune in KNON-FM to catch disc jockey Dan O's tribute. "Here's some live Stevie Ray, recorded last year in Dallas with Robert Cray," he mutters in funereal tones, pausing a few seconds before adding, "...the last solo is screaming."

I pull into a park in the South Dallas neighborhood where Stevie Ray grew up. A red pickup truck with the words "Life without You" emblazoned in white paint on the hood informs me that this is the right place. I walk toward a thicket of many flickering lights. In the distance, in the middle of a grassy meadow, a few hundred mourners sit in a circle around a huge tree. Dozens of white candles placed around the tree trunk bathe the sad faces in an eerie glow. This is no beer-guzzling, carousing hang. The mood is respectful, peaceful. Their heads bowed, some mourners hold hands in silence as the flames illuminate a series of photographs placed at the base of the great tree.

Among the pictures is a telling shot of a 15-year-old Little Stevie playing a guitar. Same posture, same attitude—even then he had "The Look." Vigil organizer Christian Brooks speaks softly of growing up with Stevie and Jimmie in Oak Cliff. A part-time drummer and full-time custom leather craftsman (he made the strap worn so proudly and for so long by Stevie Ray), he recollects a true blue friendship that began at Kimball High and continued through the years.

Suddenly, the reverential silence is shattered by a man overcome by grief. He steps into the ring of mourners, shaking as he testifies: "I grew up with Stevie Ray. And I just wanna say that I loved Stevie Ray Vaughan." He begins meekly, but gains courage and conviction at the urging of the crowd. "Now, if you don't mind, I'd like to sing a song for him." The mourners shout their approval. He closes his eyes, summons some inner reserve and belts out a psalm with sanctified intensity. Several in the crowd, tears streaming down their faces, raise their hands to the sky and praise God.

FRIDAY, AUGUST 31–DALLAS

More than 3,000 of the faithful gather at Laurel Land Memorial Park, braving 100-degree temperatures to say farewell to Stevie Ray. By noon those wearing suits are already drenched in sweat. Inside the chapel, close friends and family mourn in private. Outside, anxious photographers from AP, UPI and the local papers stand ready with telephoto lenses, waiting to snap the processional as it exits the chapel and moves the 100 yards or so to the site of the public service—near Stevie Ray Vaughan's grave. Cable networks and local TV stations are present in full force, their on-air crews trying to hold up under the intense heat.

Near the burial site are the more than 150 floral arrangements that have been sent from around the world. Several are shaped like Stevie Ray's Strat and bear his SRV logo. Off to one side, a recent photo of Stevie Ray is propped on an easel; his trademark black bolero is draped over one corner of the portrait. Nearby stands a placard: "We will cherish what you have given us and weep for the music left unplayed."

First to emerge from the chapel is Stevie Wonder. A hush comes over the crowd as he is led to a sheltered reviewing stand near the grave. The casket is placed in a white hearse, which slowly drives to the site; the mourners follow behind on foot. Jimmie and his mother, Martha, walk with the late guitarist's fiancé, Janna Lapidus. Strolling behind them, heads bowed, are Chris Layton, Tommy Shannon and Kim Wilson. Behind them are Jeff Healey and his band, a tearful Charlie Sexton, Dr. John, ZZ Top's Billy Gibbons, Dusty Hill and Frank Beard, Mark Pollack of the Charley's Guitars store in Dallas, Colin James and Charlie Comer, Stevie Ray's personal friend and publicist for the past eight years. Buddy Guy, overcome with grief, slips out of the chapel into a nearby car.

The Reverend Barry Bailey of the First United Methodist Church of Fort Worth (Stevie Ray's AA sponsor) opens the service with some personal thoughts, his rich voice booming through two huge stacks of speakers. "We're here to thank God for this man's life," he begins. "He was a genius, a superstar, a musician's musician. He captured the hearts of thousands and thousands of people. I am thankful for the impact of this man's influence on thousands of people in getting his own life together in the name of God."

Stevie Ray's close friend Bruce Miller steps to the podium and reads the "Twelve Steps to Recovery" from the Alcoholics Anonymous Big Book, placing it on the casket as he concludes. Several mourners weep openly as Nile Rodgers eulogizes Stevie Ray by recalling a tune from the *Family Style* session he had produced only a few short weeks earlier:

"In the song 'Tick Tock,' he sings the refrain, 'Remember.' And what Stevie was trying to tell all of us was, 'Remember my music. Remember how important music is to all of us. And just remember that it's a gift.' Stevie was truly touched by the hand of God. He had a powerful gift. And through his music, he can make us all remember things that are very, very important, like love and family."

His voice begins to crack with emotion as he continues. "Jimmie and Stevie made me a part of their family when we were doing the record. And I feel very, very sorry that I wasn't able to say to Stevie, to his face, 'Thank you, Stevie. Thank you for making me remember music, thank you for sharing a part of your music with me. Thank you for sharing your love with me. Thank you for making me a part of your family. Thank you for making me your brother. I'll always love you. I'll always cherish the moments that we spent together. And believe me Stevie, I'll always remember."

With that, the soulful sound of Stevie's soothing vocal on "Tick Tock" begins to pour through the speakers, touching hearts and raising goose bumps. The crowd applauds and cheers as one.

Bonnie Raitt, Jackson Browne and Stevie Wonder lead the crowd in a sing-along of "Amazing Grace." Bonnie carries the melody as the other two harmonize. When Raitt says, "Take it, Stevie," the magnificent Wonder voice, swooping and swirling around the notes with awesome, emotionally charged power, causes many in the crowd to lose control. Tears flow as his voice soars.

Finally, the mourners line up. One by one they pass the casket, some tossing flowers, religious artifacts and guitar picks as they go by. The last to pay his respects is Doug Castor, the young man who had mistakenly flown in to Austin from Pittsburgh two days earlier. He wheels himself up to the casket and says his fond farewells to Stevie Ray Vaughan.

Back at the hotel, I lie quietly on my bed, listening to a tape of an interview I had with Stevie Ray in 1988, some months after his departure from the rehab center in Marietta, Georgia. His words still ring in my ears:

"There's just a lot more reasons to live now. I can honestly say that I'm really glad to be alive today, because, left to my own devices, I would've slowly killed myself. There were a lot of things I was running from, and one of them was me. But you can't run from yourself. It may sound kind of trite, like 'No matter where you go, there you are.' But it really is true. I've made a commitment now, not for the rest of my life, but just for today. Now, each day's a new victory."

GUITAR WORLD, SEPTEMBER 1994

STEP LIVELY

Recalling the recording process of SRV's IN STEP with album producer Jim Gaines.

By Alan di Perna

"**W**E CALL IT the Wall of Doom." Veteran producer Jim Gaines laughs fondly as he recalls Stevie Ray Vaughan's pile of amps and speakers, all stacked in a big tower at Kiva Studios in Memphis and ready to record what would become the *In Step* album. Released in 1989, *In Step* was a landmark recording for the guitar virtuoso, whose life and career were sadly cut short four years ago this August. The final album from Stevie Ray Vaughan and his Double Trouble band, *In Step*, captures Vaughan and company at their musical peaks. The record contains some of the most plaintive, tearful guitar work SRV ever wrenched from his battered Strat, which sounded as though somehow it knew that it was soon to lose its best friend in the world.

In Step was the group's first—and, as it turned out, only—collaboration with Gaines, a seasoned producer with albums by Albert Collins, Santana, Steve Miller, Huey Lewis and Van Morrison to his credit. Among Gaines' earliest professional experiences was a stint at Memphis' legendary Stax Studios from 1965-68, the r&b label's wonder years. He also worked as chief engineer for Steve Cropper at the guitarist's own recording studio in Memphis. Gaines' trial by fire in the world of blues and r&b led to his developing a "capture it live" style of recording that happened to be perfectly suited to Stevie Ray's own instinctive, emotive take on the blues. Carlos Santana foresaw this compatibility and recommended Gaines to Vaughan.

"Stevie wanted to record *In Step* as live as possible," the producer recalls. "It took a while to accomplish that, mainly for technical reasons. We set up his full stage rig in the studio, so I actually had anywhere from eight to 10 amps going at any one time."

Ah yes, the aforementioned Wall of Doom. Gaines recalls that it included a Dumble amp, Marshalls, Fender Bassmen, Super Reverbs and Quad Reverbs. "We had at least four or five big Marshall and Hiwatt cabinets. We used a lot of the Hiwatt cabinets with the Dumble amps, because they're pretty clean and can take a lot of power. I had a big iso booth, and it was just Stevie and his guitars and amps in there. If we were going to cut a track, he'd show up early and spend two or three hours messing around with his amps. Between his guitar and the amps he'd basically use two Ibanez Tube Screamers and two wah-wah pedals. And then we'd use the amps to achieve different sounds. We'd use the Quads for the brighter, more metallic-sounding stuff and the Marshall for a little more crunch. The Dumbles are very powerful, clean amps. But sometimes you want some grunge to go with that, so you had to add some Marshalls to it. The Bassman would give you more low end. Each amp played its own little role in the makeup of Stevie's sound."

There was only one hitch, Gaines says: "Every day Stevie would blow up his amps! By the time he got the sound he wanted, after two or three hours of experimenting, the amps would be shot. I had [*noted amp builder/expert*] Cesar Diaz on hand, repairing amps the whole time. You have to remember three things: First, Stevie played with those big, heavy strings, second, he played real loud, and third, he tuned down a half step. Sometimes those poor amps just couldn't take those three factors all at once. I mean, he used just about the heaviest strings I've ever seen on a guitar. [*Vaughan usually used .012s—GW Ed.*]. The man had probably the strongest grip of anybody I ever met. Most guys couldn't play those strings like that. They could never do the bends."

To capture the mighty roar coming from Vaughan's Wall of Doom, Gaines used a combination of close miking on each amp cabinet and mid-distance stereo miking of the entire collective sound. Thanks to all those mics on individual amps, "Stevie's initial guitar part would go down to anywhere from eight to 10 tracks on the multi-track," Gaines details. "And sometimes I'd just have to mike the room. You could run into some weird phasing problems with the individual mics because the speakers were all reacting differently." [*A phenomenon known as "speaker damping factor"—GW Ed.*] Some of them were a little quicker than others. So what I would do was put up a stereo pair of mics in front of all the amps and try to capture where the convergence points were. I'd generally use [*Shure SM*] 57s or [*Sennheiser*] 421s and set up a pair anywhere from six to 10 feet in front of the amps, depending on the kind of sound I wanted. Then, during the mixdown, if I needed something more, I still had all the individual amps on separate tracks, so I could pull up what I needed. I was basically trying to cover my butt at all times. When you're going for live performances, the number one consideration is to get the performance down on tape. But you also try to leave yourself some options for the mixdown."

Many players would probably consider the Wall of Doom more than enough amplification for recording an album. But Gaines had two additional amps off in separate iso booths: an old stereo Gibson, one of the triangle-shaped jobbies [*In the Sixties, Gibson produced a line of stereo amps to be used in conjunction with their stereo ES-335 and ES-355 guitars—GW Ed.*] and a small Vibratone Leslie amp. "Those two amps didn't have enough power to be heard over all those other amps," Gaines explains, so I had to isolate them."

The small Leslie amp is what is responsible for Stevie Ray Vaughan's trademark chorus tone, featured on the tune "Wall of Denial." Gaines recalls that, "Stevie didn't want to use many effects in the mixing. So for chorusing effects we'd use the little Leslie amp and we'd put a VARIAC [*voltage regulator*] on it to vary the speed [*of the Leslie rotor*], so the chorusing would be in time with the song. That amp went onto a separate pair of tracks. I miked it in stereo to

get the most out of the chorus effect. If we wanted more of a chorusing sound in the mix, we'd pull up that pair of tracks. Then if we
wanted any other chorusing, the only thing Stevie would want to
use would be the old Roland Dimension D."

Because he had so many individual guitar tracks to put on
tape, Gaines suggested that *In Step* be recorded on the Mitsubishi
digital format, which provides 32 tracks as opposed to the 24-track
format of most analog machines. This suggestion met with some
initial resistance, he reports: "So what I did at our first sessions was
set up an analog machine and a digital machine side by side. I
recorded the band on both machines simultaneously. Then I played
the tracks back to the band without telling them which machine
was which, because they were very opposed to digital. No way they
were gonna like that, they said. But guess which format they picked
when I played both back? They went straight for the digital. So that's
what we used for the album."

In Step was a first for Stevie Ray Vaughan and Double Trouble
in many respects. "What a lot of people don't realize is that this is
the first album the band made after they'd gone into the [*rehabilitation*] program," says Gaines. "Their previous records had been
made under the influence of a lot of alcohol and drugs. This is the
first record they made being clean—and also the first record they
made with sort of an outside producer. So everybody was a little ner-
vous. They weren't sure what my role was, or what their role was
supposed to be."

Some of the most trying moments came when Vaughan went
to record his lead vocals, at Soundcastle in L.A., after the basic tracks
and instrumental overdubs had been completed down in Memphis.
"Stevie hated to do vocals," Gaines recalls. "He hated his voice.
Getting him to do vocals was like pulling teeth. He was very ner-
vous about his singing. So it took a while to get the vocals—a time
of coaxing and prompting and patting him on the back, saying,
'Come on, you can do it.' I've been told I worked him harder at getting vocals than anyone else had ever done, it made him a little ner-
vous. But when *In Step* came out, a lot of critics commented it had

some of the best signing he'd ever done."

While the vocals on *In Step* were overdubbed, many of the album's gut-bucket guitar solos were recorded live with the rhythm section, as part of the basic tracks. This was an area where Stevie Ray didn't need any coaxing at all. "The man could play his butt off," Gaines declares with due reverence. "I'd say anywhere between 55 to 70 percent of the solos on *In Step* were just the live tracks that Stevie cut with the band. If anything, we'd overdub the rhythm parts *behind* the solo—sort of the opposite of what you'd normally do. But if a guy is capable of playing a solo live—and Stevie certainly was—I prefer to have him go after his solo on the basic track. Because the band will follow him. They'll pick up the groove and drive it harder. Whereas if the guitarist is just playing rhythm, everyone tends to play less dynamically. And in blues, one of the most important things is to capture that natural dynamic interplay among the musicians. So we'd just cut entire performances until we agreed we had a great one."

When overdubs were necessary, for solos or other parts, Gaines tried to get them down on tape immediately after the basic track was cut, in order to retain the vibe of the original performance. Stevie was the kind of guy who could play solos all day long," says Gaines. "Every one would be different and they'd all be great. So which is the right one for the track? That was a tough call, sometimes. But a lot of the decision was up to Stevie. There were certain solos that he wanted kept. But there, too, his choice would often be dictated by the track—which solo worked best with the rhythm section."

SRV fans generally agree that one of *In Step*'s finest moments is the closing track, "Riviera Paradise." It's an inspired, sensitive performance of one of the guitarist's most introspective instrumental compositions. What isn't too well known is that this historic performance almost never made it to tape.

"To begin with, we'd hardly rehearsed that song," Gaines recalls. "And Stevie wanted to be in the right frame of mind when we cut it because it's a very intimate kind of song; it was very special to him. So about one o'clock one morning he decided he wanted to cut it. I only had eight or nine minutes left at the end of a reel of tape, but he said, 'Let's give it a shot.' I asked him how long it was going to be. He said, 'Four minutes.' So I figured, 'Okay, we should make it.'

"So he gets all set up in his iso booth with the lights turned down and with his back to both me and the band. We get into cutting the tune and it's obvious that this is a tremendous performance, but they've gone *way* over four minutes. I only have about 40 seconds of tape left and I see that we're nowhere near getting this song wrapped up. I can't really see anyone in the band because the lights are down. So I'm running around the control room like crazy, trying to get somebody's attention. Finally I make eye contact with [*drummer*] Chris Layton. I give him the 'cut' sign, showing him that the tape is running out. He looks up at Stevie, but Stevie's got his back to him. Then, all of a sudden, miraculously, Stevie turns around and looks at him. Chris gives him the cut sign and they wrap up the ending of the song. And I swear to you, as soon as they stopped we had just enough time for the notes to die down and then the tape ran off."

Two other tracks that Vaughan, Double Trouble and Gaines recorded during the '89 *In Step* sessions later surfaced on the posthumous collection *The Sky Is Crying*: "Boot Hill" is a rippling shuffle with tremendous swagger. And "Life by the Drop" poignantly documents Stevie Ray's struggles with addiction.

"We actually have two or three other songs from the *In Step* sessions that were never finished vocally," says Gaines. "But there's some great playing on them. They were new songs, and Stevie wasn't sure of the vocals. Some of them were a little too high for him, and at the time we didn't need to finish them because we already had a complete album's worth of material. They probably would have come out on a later album, if there'd only been time to bring the key down or for Stevie to concentrate on the vocals more.

As it is, Gaines is thankful he had time to finish the recordings he did with a man who will surely be remembered as one of the most influential guitarists of our era. "When you can't play guitar worth a damn yourself, it's really amazing to work with a great guitarist like that," the producer marvels. You can help guide that great talent and get some fantastic performances. You get to do in your mind what your hands can't do."

GUITAR WORLD, SEPTEMBER 1995

SOUL TO SOUL

On a blues night to remember, Eric Clapton, B.B. King, Bonnie Raitt, Buddy Guy, Robert Cray and other stars joined Jimmie Vaughan in paying tribute to their late friend and brother, Stevie Ray Vaughan.

By Alan Paul

JIMMIE VAUGHAN IS all over the stage, teaching Eric Clapton vocal cues even as he demonstrates a slinky riff for Bonnie Raitt, Robert Cray and Buddy Guy. The supergroup begins to run through a song, falling effortlessly into a deep, wide groove, when Clapton, a smile spreading across his usually stoic face, suddenly stops playing. The music trails off as, one by one, the musicians follow Clapton's gaze across the room.

B.B. King, the focus of this show-stopping attention, strides purposefully across the floor. Trailed by a guitar-case-toting valet, he ascends the stage and, like the father of the bride at a big, joyous wedding, embraces everyone in an expansive hug. He holds Vaughan in his arms a bit longer than the others, patting him three times on the back.

The valet takes Lucille out of her case and hands the guitar to King, who leans against a stool and begins to noodle away, loosening his fingers. Clapton respectfully takes a seat on a Fender Bassman directly behind B.B., as does Guy, both of them gazing reverentially at the blues patriarch.

When rehearsal resumes, it's with a new vigor. The circle is complete. The godfather has arrived. The event has been stamped with the good blueskeeping seal of approval.

Vaughan, King, Clapton, Guy and Co. are all old friends, and their presence here is, in fact, a spectacular act of friendship. They have come to Austin, Texas, from near and far to pay tribute to their fallen comrade, Stevie Ray Vaughan, who died five years ago after participating in a similar summit meeting at Alpine Valley, Wisconsin.

The Austin show, organized and hosted by Stevie's brother, Jimmie, was held May 11 in a TV studio before an invitation-only crowd of 400 and videotaped for a future television broadcast; negotiations with several networks are currently under way. An album and home video will likely follow. The line-up included everyone who shared the stage with Stevie Ray on August 26, 1990, the guitarist's final night on earth—Clapton, Guy, Cray, and Jimmie Vaughan—along with King, the slide diva Raitt, and two New Orleans keyboardists who were close with Vaughan, Dr. John and Art Neville.

"It was easy to figure out who to ask," Jimmie said before the show. "These people were Stevie's heroes and his friends. Without them, there was no tribute.

"Doing this has been in the back of my mind for a long time, but I didn't want to do it too soon—I couldn't have handled it, and I wanted it to be far enough removed that it could be a happy event, and not just sad. Most importantly, I wanted the music to be natural, because I knew that's what Stevie would have wanted."

The musical mix was, in fact, so natural that the whole event seemed more like a college reunion than a show biz extravaganza. Displays of ego were nonexistent—at least in the musicians' dealings with one another—and the artists seemed to relish their opportunity to play together. This was especially evident at rehearsals held the afternoon of the show, where spontaneous jams often broke out between takes and the arrival of every participating musician triggered a minicelebration.

"We don't see each other near as much as we'd like," Vaughan commented, "and certainly not all together. This is really a treat."

Although rehearsal time for the concert was limited, songs came together almost instantly. King, whose regal arrival occurred less than three hours before showtime, worked out "Telephone Song"—which he had never sung before—in 45 minutes, twice stopping run-throughs to hear a playback of Stevie Ray's version (from *Family Style*) on a hand-held recorder.

"I just got the tape a week ago," he explained after the show. "I just hummed through it a couple of times and tried to learn the song and figure out how I would sing it. I never even thought about the guitar part. I just tried to hear the chord progression and come up with something to play. That's how you do it; you just get in and see what you got. I really like the song, but I didn't even think about what Stevie played."

That was how Jimmie wanted it. "I told everyone that I wanted them to play like themselves," Vaughan said. "You don't ask B.B. King or Eric Clapton to do anything else, and besides it wouldn't be the right way to honor Stevie. And the only reason this whole thing is happening is because we all love Stevie. That's why I organized it, and that's why all these people came to do it."

Vaughan's sentiments were echoed by the other performers, each of whom recalled personal memories of Stevie Ray. Clapton noted that his relationship with Stevie was fogged by chemical dependency; the first time they met, he recalled, he was still in the grips of alcoholism. At their second meeting, it was Stevie Ray who was battling the demons of substance abuse. The third time, they were finally in a clear-headed position to appreciate and discuss one another's talents.

"I didn't get to see or hear Stevie play near often enough," Clapton said. "But every time I did, I got chills and I knew I was in the presence of greatness. He seemed to be an open channel and music just flowed through him. It never seemed to dry up."

"The most lasting memory I have of Stevie is his passion," said Raitt. "I don't think there's anyone who tears into a song the way he did. I think Stevie Ray was coming from some place so deep and so beautiful that there's no one you can compare him to."

Still, none other than B.B. King was prepared to make some comparisons, placing Stevie in the rarefied company of two of jazz's greatest innovators.

"When most of us play a 12-bar solo, we play maybe two choruses and the rest is all repetition," King said. "Stevie Ray was one of just a handful of musicians I've heard in my life—Charlie Parker and Charlie Christian come to mind—who weren't like that. The longer they played, the better they played. More ideas continuously happened. And that's the way Stevie was; his playing just flowed. He never had to stop to think.

"His execution was flawless, and his feeling was impeccable. He could play as fast as anyone, but no matter how fast he played, he never lost that feel. His guitar was his means of speech, and he spoke beautifully. I would say you could feel his soul. I know I did."

Buddy Guy, sitting at King's side, added simply, "He was one of the best ever. Period."

"That's right," King said. "He was a leader in what he did. Not a follower—a leader."

"I'm glad we're doing this," Guy continued. "And I'm glad we waited almost five years. I couldn't have even talked about it right afterwards. He was like family to me; when he died, I felt as bad as if I had lost my kid. And I still can't believe he's not here anymore. But he wouldn't have wanted it to be sad, because this is about the music, and he loved the music so purely."

The concert was divided into two segments, the first featuring Stevie Ray's Double Trouble—bassist Tommy Shannon, drummer Chris Layton and keyboardist Reese Wynans, with additional support from guitarist/pianist Denny Freeman—and the second, Jimmie's Tilt-a-Whirl Band, with Freeman, drummer George Rains and organist Bill Willis, supplemented by Shannon.

Jimmie Vaughan kicked the show off with a blistering attack on "Texas Flood," the Larry Davis song which helped launch Stevie's career. Head down, Strat capoed at the third fret, Jimmie played with searing intensity, all serious business. His trademark pompadour in glorious, Brylcreemed form, Jimmie stretched out, playing more extended lines than is his wont. Raitt followed with a foot-stomping romp through "Pride and Joy," turning in a limber, fluid, yet biting, slide solo with a down-and-dirty distorted tone. Next up was Robert Cray, who led the band through a distinctly Chuck Berry-flavored "Love Struck Baby," with Vaughan playing dead-on double-stops behind him. Dr. John followed with a sinuous, barrelhouse take on "Cold Shot," banging out his trebly triplets and octave bass lines with gusto.

Guy, taking the stage with one of his trademark polka-dot Strats, seemed genuinely moved, and several times appeared as if he might cry. "I felt Stevie looking down when I was playing," the guitarist explained after the show. Guy roared through his own "Mary Had a Little Lamb," which originally appeared on his *A Man and the Blues* album (Vanguard) and was covered by Stevie Ray on *Texas Flood*. The always-unenviable task of following the hyper-magnetic Guy fell on Eric Clapton, who said simply, "I'm scared," before proffering a fairly straight rendition of "Empty Arms." Clapton tipped his hat to Stevie Ray with a few direct cops and several SRV-style neck-length glissandos.

The concert's second half began with B.B. King's first appearance of the night. Both King and his beloved Lucille were in fine form on "Telephone Song," offering up streams of melodic, liquid-toned guitar work. On the coda, rhythm guitarist Vaughan stepped forward, initiating some sterling interplay between two of blues guitar's most consummately tasteful players.

Raitt and Cray returned to the stage to duet on the rollicking "Hard to Be," each of them displaying the kind of hard-driving intensity that has been lacking in their own work of late. Cray's vocals dominated the mix, but while Raitt's singing may have been a tad tentative, her playing was remarkably sure-fingered, as she peppered the song with biting slide fills. On her solo, Raitt unwinded long, languid legato lines which glided over and around the hard-charging rhythm section. Not to be outdone, Cray, eyes closed, stepped forward and released a handful of stabbing, staccato notes, which capped off a thoroughly impressive performance.

Clapton returned next, playing an inspired "Ain't Gone 'n' Give up on Love." He grabbed the slow blues by the throat and shook it with feral intensity. Playing with fire in his belly and passion in his heart, Clapton unleashed a barrage of rapid-fire, increasingly aggressive licks on his cream-colored Strat. An impressively fiery performance.

Next to return to the stage was Guy. A mesmerizing singer, he turned "Long, Long Way from Home" into a dramatic, foreboding, vocal showpiece. Starting at low volume, Guy masterfully manipulated dynamics to build from a whisper to a roar, letting out a burst of barely controlled feedback that served as a perfect metaphor for his reckless playing, which, though it often seemed on the verge of falling apart (and occasionally did), kept the crowd riveted to every note. Predictably unpredictable, Guy was the only performer to radically deviate from that afternoon's rehearsal.

Art Neville sang a moving, churchy "Life without You," the lyrics taking on poignant new meaning in his rendition: "Oh, how I miss you…the angels have waited for so long, now they have their way…take your place…fly on, fly on, fly on my friend."

The concert was gaining steam, but the real fun was just about to begin, as everyone took the stage for the much-anticipated grand finale. Vaughan, standing at center stage, launched into "Six Strings Down," a moving tribute to his brother from his own *Strange Pleasure* album. Everyone kicked in, each player finding a corner of the song and making it his or her own, with Cray firing off economical, chiming counterpoint to Raitt's stinging slide, King playing fills to Clapton's slinky three-note solo, and Guy unleashing piercing, single-note bends to answer Vaughan, who fingerpicked the main theme on his battered Strat. The sounds rose together and meshed into one glorious guitar wail, sending the song soaring into the stratosphere.

And when Vaughan, head thrown back, eyes tightly clenched,

sang "Alpine Valley, in the middle of the night/Six strings down, on the heaven-bound flight/Got a pick, a strap, guitar on his back/Ain't gonna cut the angels no slack/Heaven done called another blues stringer back home," the music was so powerfully evocative of Stevie Ray that for a lingering instant it seemed as if he might stride on stage, "Number One" Strat in hand. It was a transcendent moment—the kind one is lucky to experience a handful of in a lifetime of playing and listening to music.

"We all felt it," Jimmie Vaughan said after the show. "A really special moment passed between us all. That just happens sometimes in music. My mother and some other family and friends in the audience confirmed what I thought—they all felt it too."

But there was still much more to come. Vaughan's trio of back-up singers took the stage for "Tick Tock," a paean to world peace and universal spirituality written by Jimmie and Nile Rodgers and sung by Stevie on *Family Style.* Mono-named singer Briz took the song to church, building a gospel fervor that was picked up on by King, who launched a soaring cluster of blue notes which ascended like a mournful lamentation for Stevie Ray. As the song built to a crescendo, with Clapton playing a pungent solo, Jimmie looked upward and grinned from ear to ear.

At the conclusion of "Tick Tock," an unrehearsed jam erupted, with King playing a flurry of his trademark, heavily vibratoed licks, which Cray answered with a pithy, sharp-toned attack. Guy responded with several overbends, so absurdly wide that they cracked up Clapton, who flashed a huge cross-stage grin at Vaughan. But Guy had only just begun; he unleashed a cluster of seemingly insane notes, entering a land of total abandon where few dare to tread. But Clapton took up the challenge, answering Guy with a chorus of repeats which built to an impressive, if more controlled, frenzy. Raitt responded with spitfire slide clarions, before Jimmie literally leapt to center stage, taking over with his own unorthodox attack—percussive, staccato fingerpicking.

The song was winding down, but no one was ready for the evening to end, so Clapton took another chorus, which B.B.

answered, the two of them engaging in a call and response. Then, with the band laying out, the guitarists went round-the-clock playing unaccompanied choruses: Cray, King, Guy, Clapton, Raitt and Vaughan, a conversation between the six surviving members of blues' first family. And when it ended, the royalty still weren't quite ready to vacate the throne.

King stretched the night out for a few more glorious minutes by breaking into "When the Saints Go Marching In," evoking the spirit of a New Orleans funeral where, once the deceased is laid to rest, a marching band kicks into party mode, looking death in the eye and celebrating the beauty and delicacy of life. The song led to everyone taking another unaccompanied chorus, until the inevitable happened and this summit meeting was actually, finally, over. Hugs and handshakes broke out all over the stage. Jimmie went right for B.B., and the blues patriarch wrapped the bereaved brother in a giant bear hug at center stage as everyone crowded around and slapped their backs, joining in on a communal embrace. The evening was over, tribute had been paid. It was not hard to picture Stevie Ray Vaughan, somewhere, tipping his hat in thanks.

NUMBER ONE SONS

A Stevie Ray Vaughan Axology.
By Rudolf Schmidt

IKE MOST BLUES men, Stevie Ray Vaughan was partial to certain instruments and amps. But he wasn't above playing around. The "Number One" axe in Vaughan's life, however, was a well-worn '59 Fender Stratocaster.

"It has a 1959 body and 1961 rosewood fingerboard neck," explained Vaughan. "I had to replace the neck because the original fretboard was getting too buzzy. My guitar tech, Rene Martinez, did a wonderful job trying to preserve the original neck, but one day we looked at each other and he said, 'Unless we want to do major surgery, we really ought to find another neck.' Right around that same time I found a left-handed Strat that I really liked. In some ways I think left-handed headstocks work better."

The '59 Strat also is equipped with a left-handed (upside down) vibrato bar unit, à la Jimi Hendrix and Otis Rush. Vaughan strung the guitar with heavy gauge GHS strings (highest to lowest: .013, .015, .019 plain, .028, .038, .058), and replaced the stock frets with bass frets (which are far wider than the stock Strat frets of the Sixties) for improved grip and increased sustain.

Besides "Number One" (which was destroyed one month before Stevie Ray's death, when a piece of scenery at the Garden

State Arts Center in New Jersey crashed onto a number of SRV's guitars), Vaughan used a slew of Strats, including an off-white '61 with a custom pickguard by Martinez, and "Charley," a 1983 custom Strat that Vaughan received as a gift from the late Charley Wirz, of Charley's Guitars in Dallas, Texas. The "Charley" Strat, which can be seen on the cover of *Couldn't Stand the Weather*, features Danelectro pickups. On the back of the guitar, a simple message is engraved on the metal plate where the neck joins the body: "To Stevie From Charley. More in '84."

The unique, hollowed-out, yellow 1964 Strat (nicknamed "Lenny"), used on such classic cuts as "Lenny," "Tell Me" and "Honey Bee," was unfortunately stolen. "It was originally owned by someone in Vanilla Fudge," recalled Stevie. "It had four humbuckers in it. Charley Wirz took the humbuckers out and replaced them with a single Strat pickup in the neck position. It would probably be hard to recognize now. That was the first guitar Charley gave to me, and it meant a lot."

Whenever the Texas bluesman was in a mellow mood, he was known to play a Gibson Johnny Smith model arch-top electric/acoustic jazz guitar. This instrument can be heard on "Stang's Swang."

SRV began his recording career using the combination of Marshall 2 x 12 combos (for clean sounds) and Fender Vibroverbs/Fender Super Reverbs (for distortion) heard on *Texas Flood*. By 1984, he found his signature tone in two Fender Vibroverbs and a Howard Dumble 150-watt Steel String Singer.

His signal processing gear was deceptively simple—an Ibanez Tube Screamer (for volume and gain boost), a Vox wah-wah pedal (or two, as on "Say What!") and, occasionally, a Fuzzface and Octavia. The rotating speaker sound (like the Leslie cabinet of a Hammond B-3 organ) on "Cold Shot" was produced by a vintage (late-Sixties) Fender Vibratone Unit.

"I have the Tube Screamer, a wah and the Leslie on my pedal board," explained Vaughan. "The whole system can be activated or deactivated with a simple on/off switch. When I do a song like

'Third Stone from the Sun,' I can't control the feedback with the effects on, so I switch 'em all off and then kick it back when I'm done."

Guitar World, September 1997

PRIDE & JOYS

Guitar tech Rene Martinez delivers the final word on SRV's gear

By Andy Aledort

DURING THE LAST five years of his life, the late great Stevie Ray Vaughan relied on one man to maintain the gear that helped him produce his devastating guitar sound, and to ensure that everything under the hood of his cherished main guitar, "Number One," was runnin' smooth. That man was guitar tech Rene Martinez, whose devotion to his late boss is apparent both from the diligence with which he served him and the respect he accords his memory. In the following interview with Martinez, *Guitar World* delivers the most comprehensive account of Stevie's gear ever to appear in print. Here is the *inside* inside track on every last detail of one of the greatest guitar tones ever produced by man or bluesman.

GUITAR WORLD: When did you first work with Stevie Ray Vaughan?
RENE MARTINEZ: It was in 1985—I worked with him from 1985 until August of 1990.
GW: What was Stevie playing when you began working with him?
MARTINEZ: When I came on board, we were in the studio in Dallas, recording the album *Soul to Soul* (Epic, 1985). At that time, his primary guitar was Number One, the beat-up '59 Strat that he was

most noted for.

GW: It is widely held that Number One's body, neck and pickups are all from different years. Is this true?

MARTINEZ: The body and the neck are from the same vintage year. It is often the case that a guitar's neck is about three months older than its body. Number One may have had the biggest neck of any Strat ever made. Fender rated the necks in terms of size with the designations A, B, C or D; D is the largest. That neck was definitely a D neck. It had a rosewood fingerboard, with jumbo frets.

GW: Stevie always said that he preferred Gibson Jumbo bass frets over all others.

MARTINEZ: Yeah, well, guitar players have a tendency to pick up whatever words that they hear about something, and, as a tech, I can only go, "Oh, okay, sure. Why not." [*chuckles*] It's possible that the guitar was refretted with Gibson frets that were referred to as "jumbo," but they were not really bass frets. I always speak of fretwire in terms of "jumbo" or "medium," and I did not use Dunlop 6150 wire or whatever on Stevie's guitars. The fact is, I didn't use any one particular fret wire, but the thickest and highest I could find with tangs that would fit in the preexisting slots without hurting the fingerboard.

GW: Did Stevie ever voice any particular preferences regarding the wire, like, for instance, that he wanted a wire that was higher than it was wide?

MARTINEZ: Yes, he did. He liked his fretwire as tall as it possibly could be. With the heavy gauge strings he used, he wanted to be able to really dig into the fingerboard, so height was the primary concern. I never relied on measurements; I went for a wire with the tallest bead and the smallest tang.

GW: Regarding the neck/body thing, it's always been reported that the body dated from an earlier year than the neck.

MARTINEZ: Here's the true story: The first time I ever saw Number One was at a music store in Dallas called Charley's Guitar Shop, where I worked. Charley Wirz, who is now deceased, was the owner, and he and I worked together to make the store happen. I first encountered Number One in about 1980, when it needed some work and Stevie brought it in for Charley to look at.

You can tell how old Strats are by taking the necks off, because the date is stamped on the end of the neck, where the neck joins the body. The year "1962" was stamped on the neck, and the year "1962" was written in the body cavity, as it usually was on Fender guitars of that vintage. Now, Stevie always referred to the guitar as a '59. So I looked at Charley and said, "Why does Stevie call this a '59?" It wasn't until a while later, in a talk I had with Stevie, when he said to me, "Well, if you look on the back of the pickups, '1959' is hand-written on there." Back in those days, it was a common practice to hand-write the year on the back of the pickups, so ever since Stevie saw the 1959 on there, he started calling it a '59. Charley added, "Look, it's his guitar, and it's not our place to say otherwise." That was fine with me, so, as far as I'm concerned, it was a '59. That's the bottom line.

GW: Was the neck a "slab-board" from '62? [*A "slab-board" is a rosewood fretboard that is flat on the underside, where it is joined to the maple neck, as opposed to a "veneer" fretboard, which is curved on the underside.—GW Ed.*]

MARTINEZ: No, that neck had a "veneer" fretboard. All of Stevie's other rosewood-board guitars were slab-boards, however.

GW: Aside from the black pickguard, which obviously was added later, was that guitar 100 percent stock?

MARTINEZ: Yes, all except for the five-way toggle switch that Stevie had installed, and the lefty tremolo arm.

GW: What is the origin of the lefty tremolo arm?

MARTINEZ: The lefty tremolo arm was installed in the guitar before I met Stevie, and I don't know where the alteration was done—it was somewhere in southeast Texas. He needed to have his tremolo arm repaired, but they didn't have a right-handed tremolo in stock. All they had was the lefty tremolo, so he had that installed instead.

GW: So it was really serendipity; he wasn't looking to put a lefty tremolo on there.

MARTINEZ: It was a little bit of both. He probably thought, "Hey, it's the only one they've got, and it would be just like Hendrix. How long would it take to put this on?" The body had to be routed slightly to fit the lefty tremolo in there, and the other side of the tremolo slot was plugged with a piece of wood.

GW: Did Stevie insist on having lefty tremolos installed on all of his guitars?

MARTINEZ: Oh, no. He just had it on that one particular guitar, and he never stressed a need to have it on any other guitar.

GW: Was that tremolo assembly originally gold-plated, as it appears to be in so many photos of Number One?

MARTINEZ: No, it was originally chrome. The gold-plating was my idea. When I started working with Stevie, we became, somehow, very close, almost immediately. I felt a lot closer to Stevie than just as a "business" friend. When he asked me to work for him, a cousin of mine in Los Angeles had access to all kinds of Fender parts. I asked him to find me everything he could in gold. I bought it all, and I went to see Steve and showed it to him. I said that we should color Number One with gold. He was ecstatic over the idea. That was in late '85 or early '86.

GW: Were you able to get gold-plated tremolo arms, too?

MARTINEZ: I got gold-plated everything! [*laughs*] We were staying at some hotel somewhere, and I had all of these gold-plated parts in a bag in my pocket. Stevie was downstairs in the lounge, and I sat next to him at the bar and pulled out the bag. His jaw just dropped, and he said, "Golly, I can't believe you got this!" So I took just about everything off Number One and replaced it all with gold.

GW: Did Stevie break a lot of tremolo arms, like when he would swing the guitar around by the arm at the end of "Third Stone from the Sun" or "Voodoo Chile"?

MARTINEZ: Yes, he broke a tremendous amount of arms all the time! Oftentimes, I couldn't get the broken piece of the tremolo arm out of the inertia block [*the piece of the bridge assembly that the tremolo arm screws into*], so I'd have to replace that, too. Stevie liked to use all five springs for the tremolo, which put extra strain on the arm.

GW: Did Stevie ever specify a preference for a certain type of tremolo-arm block?

MARTINEZ: No. We used old ones and new ones, but it had to be a left-handed one for Number One. I knew some people at Fender, and through them and the people I'd met at numerous guitar shows, I was always able to get lefty blocks when I needed them. I still have a few left today.

I also tried a bunch of different types of tremolo arms. The stainless steel ones were good, because they would last a little longer than those made of alloy. A trick I developed was to put a bit of cotton inside the arm hole so the bullet—the screw end of the tremolo arm—wouldn't bottom out in there, and would be easier to remove the next time the arm broke.

GW: That's thinking ahead.

MARTINEZ: Yeah, I had to do that, because I knew he'd break another arm sooner or later—probably sooner. We were in Italy once, on a Sunday, and the night before, he'd broken his tremolo arm, the very last one we had—and we had a show that Sunday night. This was on Number One, and I thought, "What am I going to do?!" I wanted to send a runner out looking for a store, and everybody looked at me and said, "There are no stores open in Italy on Sunday!" So, I took the broken arm, which happened to be made of stainless steel, thank God, and took the knob-end and screwed it into the inertia block. Then I bent the arm in approximately the right place, and put the knob back on the broken end. And there was a tremolo arm! It was a little shorter than it should have been [*laughs*], but it worked! At least until Monday came, which was the next day.

GW: Did he go a little easy on the arm at that night's show?

MARTINEZ: Oh, no! It was full-throttle, 'cause Monday would come tomorrow. My job was to make it happen for Sunday. Many times he would look at me and say, "I don't know how you're pulling these rabbits out of your hat, but keep doing it!"

GW: Another idiosyncrasy of Stevie's was his habit of putting a bit of wire insulation around the string where it came out of the tremolo block, in order to prevent string breakage. Was that something he'd been doing all along, or was that your contribution?

MARTINEZ: That was my contribution. I needed to come up with a way of cutting down on the amount of broken strings—he broke a lot of 'em. The strings come out of the inertia block and dig into the bridge plate, get caught on an edge and break. Besides using the wire insulation, I would also use a Dremel Moto-drill to smooth out where the string passed through the bridge plate, and that helped, too. Doing all of that worked out real well, in fact—Stevie could go 15 shows with the same set of strings, and not break a single one. Only those results let me know that what I was doing was really working.

GW: Stevie was a very physical player, especially with his right hand.

MARTINEZ: Oh, yeah. He had very strong hands. I can't say that he was abusive to the guitar; that's just the way that he played.

GW: I've also heard that he preferred bone nuts, which you hand-made for him.

MARTINEZ: Yes, that's true. I always told him that for the best sound, bone or ivory for the nut was the only way to go. The first one I made for him impressed Stevie very much. Of the many things that I suggested to him, some he'd like, some he didn't like. But he was always thankful that I was around to help him find the tone he was looking for. To me, then and now, my job is to make the guitar player sound the best that he can, and to create a situation where he doesn't have to worry about all of the little crap—where all he has to do is go out on the stage and play. I don't want to make a guitar player sound like me; I want to help him sound like him, and to tell me the things that he isn't happy with. My job is to take care of those things, so all he has to think about is playing. That has always been my whole intent. With Stevie, I think I helped out in a lot of little ways.

GW: One reason that guitar players love old Stratocasters, I believe, is their curved fretboard radius. Did Stevie ever voice a preference for one fretboard radius over another?

MARTINEZ: Well, each of his guitars had its own distinct radius. Whenever I had to refret a guitar, which was quite often, I had to plane the fingerboard. This takes some of the radius out of the board, making it somewhat flatter. I did this very lightly, just enough so that the frets would be even; I wouldn't take off any more than a few thousandths of an inch. If there was any difference in the radius after a fret job, Stevie never indicated that he was unhappy with it. Stevie never even expressed any preference for one type of fretboard radius over another, to tell you the truth. But he kept his action very high, so there was no way for him to "fret out," no matter what the radius was. He liked a high action because of the tone he got with it. He did tune down one half step, with the low E at Eb, which gave him a little leeway with the high action and heavy strings. When he picked a string, he liked for there to be a nice, clean ring to the note, and that's what high action gives you.

GW: Did you need to keep the truss rods in Stevie's guitars extra tight, in order to help the necks stand up to the heavy strings?

MARTINEZ: Oh, yes; I had to keep an eye on all of the guitars all of the time. With any kind of weather change, hot or cold, I always had to make a tweak here and a tweak there. I always made sure the four bolts that hold the neck onto the body were tight, and I had to move the necks back into place when they shifted. This was a daily thing, a way of ensuring that everything was working properly. Even with all of the preventive maintenance, though, sometimes something would just give, and I'd be back to repairing or finding more parts to use as replacements.

GW: Did you ever have a truss rod break in any of his necks?

MARTINEZ: No—I made sure that would never happen. There are simple things one can do to prevent it.

GW: Did those original 1959 pickups stay in Number One through-out Stevie's career?

MARTINEZ: Unbelievably, they did. Just a few months before Stevie passed away, to make sure everything was fine I opened up the cavity and took one of the pickup covers off. I was amazed to see that the pickup itself was bowed, going towards the body! When I looked further, they were all bowed like this. I thought, "I can't believe he hasn't broken a winding on any of these pickups!" I cleaned off all of the dust and put the guitar back together, and when I saw Stevie, I told him what I'd seen. I said, "If you're going to be riding Number One again..."—like you've seen him do on stage, when he put his entire weight on the guitar, and would jump on top of it—"…those pickups are going to be gone. I don't know if I'll be able to repair it, and that tone you love is going to be history!" I think he babied it for about three shows, and then gave up and went back to doing what he always did.

GW: Number One always had a very distinctive tone, a "growl" that none of his other guitars had.

MARTINEZ: It sure did. That was a sound you could rely on.

GW: Were the pots in the guitar of the stock 250 k variety?

MARTINEZ: Yes. In the last tone position, we installed a push-push pot, because we were trying to cut down on the hum from the single-coil pickups. I added a dummy coil in there to keep the guitar from buzzing, plus some different value capacitors so the tone would stay as close to the original sound as possible. That was about it. I changed some of the pots that had worn out or broken.

GW: When replacing a saddle, did you always use Fenders?

MARTINEZ: Yes. Sometimes they'd be of a different vintage, but it always had to be a Fender because that's the only kind that would fit the bridge assembly.

GW: One last question about Number One: Was it an alder body?

MARTINEZ: Yes. Stevie had his name inscribed on the back of it and had a label on the front; he also had the sticker under the bridge that said "custom," that he picked up somewhere. I used to buy all of the "SRV" decals for the pickguard at truck stops. We'd stop at one after a show just for fun, and I'd buy the reflective S's, R's and V's. As he'd wear them out, I'd cut the edging off the letters and put the new ones on.

GW: When you first saw the guitar, were white "SRV" letters affixed to the upper horn of the guitar?

MARTINEZ: Yeah, he had some kind of plastic letters glued on there, but eventually they all came off from the fast strumming, the fanning, he did with the pick. He could fan so fast that he actually burned some red from a red pick into the white pickguard, on the guitar he called "Butter," which was butterscotch colored. It looked like it had melted into the pickguard, and was fused on there!

Unbelievable, huh? [*laughs*] I'd never seen anything like that before.

GW: Another side effect from the heavy strumming was the big spot of raw wood visible on Number One, right above the pickguard at the neck pickup. Why does that spot look a lot lighter in some pictures than in others?

MARTINEZ: When bits of the wood wore away, at first the spot would look very light-colored and raw. But the more that spot dried out, and the more hand oils wore into it, the darker it became. So what you're seeing, basically, are different shades of raw.

GW: Let's talk about his other main road guitars. One of my favorites was the red Strat, which he logically called "Red." What's the reason for the black that's all around the edges of that guitar?

MARTINEZ: Back in the days when Fender had a custom order for a specific color, whoever was the head shop guy would run into the custom shop and yell, "Hold it, we just got an order for a red one!" And they'd say, "Well, shoot, we just finished painting all of the bodies sunburst," which was the stock finish. And the head shop guy would say, "Grab that sunburst one over there and paint it red!" So what you see is the sunburst coming through the red finish, where the red paint has worn off.

GW: Did Stevie have that guitar when you first worked for him?

MARTINEZ: Yes. He bought it from Charley Wirz, in about 1984. That guitar was a '62 with a slab-board rosewood neck, and it was 100 percent stock.

GW: At some point, a left-handed neck with a large, Fender-type headstock was put on that guitar, correct?

MARTINEZ: Yeah. In 1986, somebody came up to Stevie and gave him a left-handed neck as a gift. That was a bogus neck, however—it was not a real vintage Fender neck. It was rosewood, and it had a Fender decal on it. This neck stayed on the guitar until July of '90 when, at the Garden State Arts Center in New Jersey, the stantion fell and broke it and the neck that was on Number One. Then Fender sent us two brand new necks to help get us through the tour. "Red" still has that new Fender neck.

GW: I interviewed Stevie just prior to the release of *Family Style*, and he told me that he'd retired the original neck from Number One, and had replaced it with the neck from "Butter." It was this, he said, which was broken when the stantion fell on Number One.

MARTINEZ: That's not exactly right. The neck that was on Number One when the piece of staging fell on it was the original neck from "Red"; sadly, it was destroyed. Today, the original Number One neck and Number One body are back together, in the possession of Stevie's brother, Jimmie Vaughan.

The reason we retired the Number One neck was that it had been refretted so many times, there was hardly any board left. I told Stevie that unless we did some real serious work on it, I wouldn't be able to refret it any more. He said, "Well, what are we going to do?" I told him that we had the spare neck from "Red."

GW: What's the story behind the yellow guitar that had only a single neck pickup on it, and which had the letters "SRV" pasted under the strings?

MARTINEZ: That particular guitar was given to Stevie by Charley Wirz, with just the one pickup on there, and single volume and tone controls. That Stratocaster was brought into our store by some guy who pulled up in a Cadillac. The car was towing a trailer; inside there was a passenger, fast asleep, who had his feet hanging out of the window—like something you'd see in a bad movie. The driver gets out and says he needs some cash 'cause he needs to get to New York City, and he starts bringing in all these guitar cases and amplifiers that are all numbered and labeled. The guy turned out to be the guitar player from [*Sixties psychedelic rock band*] Vanilla Fudge, Vince Martell.

He sold that yellow Strat to Charley, and when we opened it up, we saw that the whole cavity was wiped clean—it had been routed and re-routed so many times that there was hardly any wood left in there. The guy said that it had been cut out for a "shitload of humbuckers!" [*laughs*] It was very light. And the paint was not original; we painted it yellow to give to Stevie. That was in '83 or '84.

GW: Did Stevie use that guitar throughout his career?

MARTINEZ: No, because it was stolen from him in 1987, and it was never found. If anyone out there knows where it is, please come forward!

GW: What's the story behind the maple-neck vintage Strat, the one he dubbed "Lenny"?

MARTINEZ: That was a brown-stain finish on natural wood, with a butterfly tortoise-shell emblem inlaid in the body, down at the lower bout. The maple neck was relatively new, and the body had a three-ply white pickguard on it. The electronics were all old and stock. I don't know how he acquired that guitar; I never asked and he never told me. He named the guitar after his wife; they were later divorced.

GW: Is the only other vintage Strat Stevie had the one he called "Butter"?

MARTINEZ: Yes. We were at some gig somewhere, back in '87, and the sponsors were going to give that guitar away as a promotion. Stevie saw the guitar, picked it up, and really liked it. He said, "Gosh, you guys are gonna give this away? Can I buy it?" So they sold it to Stevie, and used some other guitar for the giveaway. "Butter" was a '61, with a slab-board rosewood neck. That's a really good guitar, and it was 100 percent stock. That weird looking, reddish, wood-grainy pickguard is something I cut out of a larger piece of plastic that I had.

GW: Another signature guitar of Stevie's was the custom-made one that had his name inlaid into the fretboard.

MARTINEZ: That's called a Hamiltone, built by a young kid named John Hamilton, who had been making some guitars for Billy Gibbons of ZZ Top. Billy had the guy make the guitar for Stevie, for Billy to give to Stevie as a gift.

GW: Did Stevie love this guitar?

MARTINEZ: He liked it, but he didn't particularly like the tone of it too much. The body was a two-piece, with well-figured maple, and had a neck-through-the-body design. I wound up buying some vintage Fender pickups to put in that guitar, so he could play it more often. The fretboard on the guitar is flatter than a typical Strat's; it's still curved, but it is flatter. The fretboard is made of ebony, with his name inlaid in abalone.

GW: I heard a rumor that that guitar now belongs to Kenny Wayne Shepherd.

MARTINEZ: It may; I don't know anything about that. There was a guy that was going around saying that he'd bought Stevie Ray Vaughan's Hamiltone guitar at a guitar show, and it became apparent to me that John Hamilton was making more Stevie Ray Vaughan guitars! This guy said to me, "You mean this isn't really Stevie's guitar?" And I said, "Yeah, right, like Jimmie's going to sell you the original." I don't think so.

GW: Another road guitar of Stevie's was the one with the lipstick pickups. What's the story behind that guitar?

MARTINEZ: That guitar was made for Stevie by Charley Wirz and me, from different parts we had. Charley had bought a whole bunch of old chrome Danelectro pickups, the ones we refer to as "lipstick" pickups. The body is made out of alder, and the neck is maple with an ebony fingerboard. We painted it with a trick paint we called "flip-flop," which makes the guitar look like different colors when seen from different angles. I was into trick car paints when I was a teenager, and I said, "Let's do something strange with this guitar." We painted the back of the neck, the headstock and the body, and the neck had the "Charley's Guitars" logo on it. On the neck plate was engraved "This guitar was presented to Stevie Ray Vaughan by Charley Wirz." It also said "More in '84," which was the year Charley gave the guitar to Stevie. The guitar has a non-tremolo bridge, with a single volume and a single tone control.

GW: That guitar had a very intense sound.

MARTINEZ: Oh yeah. It was like razor blades.

GW: What string gauges did Stevie usually go for?

MARTINEZ: From high to low, it was usually .013, .015, .019, .028, .038, .058. Sometimes he'd use a slightly lighter high E string, like a .012 or .011. The very last set of strings he used was .011, .015, .019, .028, .038, .058. And he always tuned down one half step.

GW: Okay, now let's get into the amplifiers. Stevie always said that his setup was a combination of Marshalls, Fenders and Dumbles. Can you be more specific?

MARTINEZ: Back in '85, Stevie would use two "blackface" Fender Super Reverbs plus a 150-watt Dumble Steel String Singer, which was a head with a 4 x 12 Dumble bottom, fitted with four 100-watt EVs. He also had another Dumble 4 x 12 bottom with another 150-watt Dumble head, though sometimes that would change. Often, he'd use a 200-watt Marshall Major head with the second 4 x 12 Dumble bottom. If he used a Marshall head, it was always a Major. The Marshall and the Dumble were two different sounds, but essentially yielded the same amount of power.

GW: What kind of tubes does the Steel String Singer use?

MARTINEZ: 6550s. Stevie never mentioned, though, that he preferred one type of tube over another. We would also run a "blackface" Fender Vibroverb, with one 15-inch speaker, that would power the Leslie-type Fender Vibratone cabinet with the rotating speaker inside.

GW: Did Stevie ever use actual Leslie cabinets on the road?

MARTINEZ: No. Only our keyboard player, Reese Wynans, would use those; Stevie always used the Fender Vibratone. We would carry three blackface Vibroverbs with us on the road, in case he blew out a speaker in one, which he did very often.

GW: What was Stevie's amp configuration live?

MARTINEZ: Two blackface Super Reverbs—each one loaded with four 10-inch EV speakers—the Dumble head driving a 4 x 12, the Marshall Major driving another 4 x 12, and a Vibroverb driving the Vibratone. All of these amps ran at the same time.

GW: Did he have specific volume settings for each of these amplifiers? Were they all on 10?

MARTINEZ: [*laughs*] They would always start out at about 7 or 7 1/2, but by the end of the show they'd all be at 10. He did this thing we called "the roll," where he'd take his hand and roll over all of the knobs, turning them all up to 10 with one quick move. He always did that for the last song, which usually was "Voodoo Chile." It wasn't at the very beginning of the song; he'd always do it at some point during the song, when he was really getting into it.

GW: Were there any specific modifications done to his amplifier heads?

MARTINEZ: No real modifications. Parts were replaced as they wore out. He may have had some things done before I came on board, but, as far as I know, the amps were not modified. If we blew out a transformer, which did happen, they'd be replaced by another of the same value.

GW: Did you have to spend a lot of time fitting his amplifiers for tubes?

MARTINEZ: Oh God, you wouldn't have believed the inventory I had! Not just the tubes, but the speakers! I had cases and cases of speakers that we carried with us on the road. I had back-ups for my back-ups!

GW: Did he blow out a lot of speakers?

MARTINEZ: It was more a case of him not liking the way a cabinet sounded on a particular day. He didn't want to hear me say, "Oh, I'll call EV tomorrow and get them to send me some new speakers." He wanted all of the speakers changed right then. Sometimes, this would happen minutes before a show. I'd run over to my case of speakers and throw a new one in there and take the old one out, which was never an old speaker, anyway. I'd send these back to EV to be rebuilt, and they'd say, "But it still has that new car smell!" [*laughs*] But they would rebuild everything because they wanted to keep his account.

GW: How many Phillips-head drill bits did you wear out?

MARTINEZ: Well, think about this: Four speakers per Super Reverb, that's eight right there. Then there are two 4 x 12s, that's another eight; and one 15-inch for the Vibroverb. So that's 17 speakers, and I had spares for each one of those, plus spares for each one of the spares. That's how many speakers I carried with me on the road, every day.

As far as tubes are concerned, I bought them left and right. 6550s, 6L6s, 12AX7s, 12AY7s—a total inventory. I had hundreds of vacuum tubes in my wood box. Strings? I had hundreds of sets! Picks? Hundreds of picks! I was a store on wheels, and was buying things at stores every chance I got.

GW: Did Stevie ever specify a preference for one type of tube over another, like Mullards or RCAs?

MARTINEZ: I told him which ones I really liked, and I think he became aware of the best ones for his sound. He knew each had a different sound, but he couldn't tell you that a GE was better than a Phillips, for example. I prefer Phillips 6L6s, Phillips 12AX7s and GE 6550s.

GW: The first time I saw Stevie live was in '84, and he had a huge Plexiglas wall set up in front of his amplifiers. What was the story with that?

MARTINEZ: He used that Plexiglas wall all the way through until the end, though there were some shows where we didn't need to use it. We had to use that Plexiglas wall because he played so loud that he was killing the people in the front of the audience, including the house engineers. The wall was used to reflect the sound back towards the amps and away from the audience.

GW: He used to venture in between that wall and his amps to get some hellacious feedback.

MARTINEZ: [*laughs*] He used to say that he liked to go in there so he could feel the wind ruffle through his pants! We were playing at this place called Chastain Park, in Atlanta, Georgia—a real hob-nob place where all the rich people used to go—and the maximum decibel level there was 95. They told Stevie at the soundcheck, "Turn this thing down now or we're gonna cut you off!" He looked at me and said, "We've got to do something!" I took this big cover to a monitor board that was on wheels—it was about 4 feet by 8 feet—and rolled it in front of the wall of amps. It was the only thing we had, because we didn't have the Plexiglas yet. When I wheeled that thing out, he said, "What in the world are you doing?" And I said, "Well, you said to hurry up and do something, so here it is!" And it worked.

GW: What pedals did Stevie use?

MARTINEZ: He always used an Ibanez Tube Screamer, starting with the original first-issue ones [*TS-808*]. He'd then move on to the new versions as they came out, so he also used the TS-9 and the TS-10 Classic. His wah of preference was always old original Vox wah-

wahs from the Sixties. When I first started working with him, he had a Univibe in his pedal setup, but he was having some problems with it, and didn't use it for very long. One day, it was just gone. Eventually, he settled on the final setup, which was an Ibanez Tube Screamer TS-10, a Vox wah-wah, a vintage Dallas-Arbiter Fuzz Face and a Tycobrahe Octavia.

The first Octavias we used were the Roger Mayer models that look like a spaceship. Then Cesar Diaz, who was working with us on the road, found three old Tycobrahe Octavias, brand-new in the box. He wound up using those because he really liked the way they sounded. At the time, he paid about $200 apiece for them. They were, undoubtedly, the best I've ever heard.

We had a lot of trouble with the Fuzz Faces because the transistors would die on us. We'd change them, but they'd just die again. Finally, Cesar Diaz came up with some circuitry based on the Fuzz Face but with some improvements, and it was very good. We put that circuitry into a Dallas-Arbiter body that I had, and when Stevie's died, I gave him this modified one to use, which I thought sounded great. That's the one he used until he passed.

GW: What kind of splitter box did he use?

MARTINEZ: It was just a diecast aluminum junction box with one input for the guitar signal coming from his last pedal, and six outs which went to each amplifier. He already had the splitter box when I came to work for him. There was no preamp in the box, and we never had a problem with the load being diminished in any way. There were some resistors in there to keep the noise down, but that was about it. I've still got that original one.

GW: Anything we forgot to cover?

MARTINEZ: Well, he always played with his pick upside down, and his pick of preference was a Fender Medium.

GW: One last question: What's happening with you, guitarwise?

MARTINEZ: I'm starting my own mail-order business, and I'll be selling tubes, polishes, cords and some other specific products. I'm going to offer the best that there is, because even though I always expect to get the best when I go to a music store, I rarely can find it. I don't have any secrets to hold out, and I do have a lot of experience to draw from. My new company is called Orimar Productions, and I'll be manufacturing guitar-related products of the professional grade. This is a mail-order business starting this July. People interested should feel free to contact me at (972) 662-2825. I'm in the process of setting up the web site now.

GUITAR WORLD, AUGUST 1992

SRV'S COMPLETE RECORDED WORKS

AS A LEADER:
The Sky Is Crying (Epic, 1991)
Family Style (Epic, 1990) with Jimmie Vaughan
In Step (Epic, 1989)
Live Alive (Epic, 1986)
Soul to Soul (Epic, 1985)
Couldn't Stand the Weather (Epic, 1984)
Texas Flood (Epic, 1983)

AS A SIDEMAN:
With Jennifer Warnes:
Famous Blue Raincoat (Cypress, 1986. Now available on Polydor.)

With Bob Dylan:
Under the Red Sky (Columbia, 1990)

With Marcia Ball:
Soulful Dress (Rounder, 1989)

With Bill Carter:
Loaded Dice (CBS, 1988)

With A.C. Reed:
I'm in the Wrong Business (Alligator, 1987)

With James Brown:
Gravity (Scotti Bros., 1986)

With Don Johnson:
Heartbeat (Epic, 1986)

With Roy Head:
Living for a Song (Texas Crude, 1985)

With Lonnie Mack:
Strike Like Lightning (Alligator, 1985)
With Bennie Wallace:
Twilight (Blue Note, 1985)
With David Bowie:
Let's Dance (EMI, 1983)
With Johnny Copeland:
Texas Twister (Rounder, 1983)

COMPILATIONS:

Back to the Beach (Columbia, 1987)
Blues Explosion (Atlantic, 1984)
A New Hi (1971, a compilation of Dallas bands)

SINGLES:

"First We Take Manhattan" (with Jennifer Warnes)
"Living in America" (with James Brown)
"Other Days"/"Texas Clover" (with Paul Ray and the Cobras)
"My Song"/"Rough Edges" (with W.C. Clark and the Cobras)
"Pipeline"/"Love Struck Baby" (with Dick Dale)

GUITAR SCHOOL, APRIL 1997

PLAYING WITH FIRE

Picking apart the finer points of Stevie Ray Vaughan's musical genius.

By Andy Aledort

MPOSSIBLE AS IT seems, 15 years have passed since the world first became aware of the intensely soulful, blues-drenched guitar playing of the late, great Stevie Ray Vaughan. Vaughan's stature as one of the greatest guitarists ever has only grown in the years since his death on August 27, 1990, at the age of 35. His influence on the way today's guitarists approach and play the instrument is immeasurable; it is apparent in the playing of guitarists in a wide range of styles, from the blues of Kenny Wayne Shepherd, to the alterna-pop of Pearl Jam's Mike McCready, to the far-out heavy rock sounds of Smashing Pumpkins' Billy Corgan. Every young blues guitarist coming up today stands in the long shadow cast by Stevie Ray's substantial contributions to the art of blues guitar. His larger-than-life playing style—not to mention *sound*—brought blues to more people around the globe than any other guitarist of his generation.

In the seven years since his death, Vaughan's unfathomably rich legacy has been left to his family, fans and fellow musicians to celebrate and carry forth. It is a legacy that is equal parts grace, grit and virtuosity; everyone who knew Vaughan knew him first as a wonderful human being, and there's no doubt that he couldn't have played the blues with as much determined emotion as he did were he not a deeply sensitive, caring person.

Let's first examine the tools of Vaughan's trade: His guitars were stock Fender Stratocasters, specifically Strats from the early Sixties. His main guitar, the beat-up sunburst with the black pickguard, which he lovingly referred to as "No. 1," was a bit of a mongrel: The "slab-board" rosewood neck was dated 1959, while the body was dated 1962. Vaughan bought the guitar in 1973 and it remained his main guitar through his entire career. (In 1989, this '59 neck was retired, as it had been refretted so many times it had become unusable. Vaughan replaced it with the neck from his 1960 cream-colored Strat, but, about six weeks before his death, this neck was crushed in a freak accident at New Jersey's Garden State Arts Center.)

The only modification he routinely made to these instruments was his choice of frets: Because of the heavy gauge strings Vaughan preferred—generally .013, .016, .019, .028, .038, .056—he replaced the small vintage Fender frets with Gibson Jumbo bass frets (virtually the largest frets available at the time). The combination of these strings with these frets, plus the standard practice of tuning down one half step (à la Jimi Hendrix), contributed greatly to the massive guitar sound integral to the Stevie Ray Vaughan experience. Vaughan protégé Kenny Wayne Shepherd uses an identical setup in his pursuit of a similarly *brutal* tone, as do many other blues guitarists today.

For amplification, Vaughan usually employed a three-amp type setup, combining 100- and 200-watt Marshalls, 150- and 300-watt Howard Dumble Steel String Singers, and a variety of old Fenders, such as Vibroverbs, Super Reverbs and Bassmans. He definitely preferred vintage amps; all of *In Step* was recorded with the same 1959 Fender Bassman. His pedal setup consisted of a vintage Vox Wah, a vintage Fuzz Face distortion pedal, a first-issue Ibanez Tube Screamer, and an Octavia. Sometimes, he'd use two wahs together (as on "Say What!," from *Soul to Soul*), or even two Tube Screamers together. But, of course, the most important ingredient in Vaughan's sound was the man himself.

Let's start at the beginning with the first cut from Vaughan's debut album, *Texas Flood*, "Love Stuck Baby." On this straight-ahead rocker, Vaughan pumps out driving rhythm guitar figures in the grand Chuck Berry tradition. **FIGURE 1** illustrates a 12-bar verse rhythm guitar figure along these same lines. This part is made up of root-fifth and root-sixth two-note chords through the first eight bars. In bars 9 and 10, Vaughan incorporates a "cowboy" type dominant seventh voicing for the E7 chord, and switches back to root-fifth and root-sixth chords in bar 11. The same chord voicings are used for the bridge progression: D-A-D-E7, which is played twice.

FIGURE 1

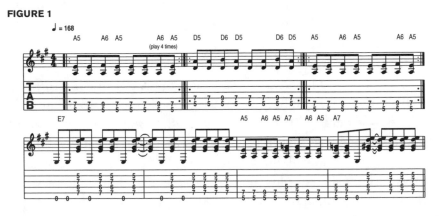

On the "Love Struck Baby" chorus, Vaughan adds an interesting seventh chord voicing to the mix, as in bars 1, 3 and 5 of **FIGURE 2**. To properly fret this chord, which first appears as A7 at the end of bar 1, barre the index finger across the low E, A and D strings at the fifth fret, and fret the E note, fifth string/seventh fret, with the ring finger. Use this same fingering for the D7 chord in bar 3. This great-sounding chord pops up on a few other SRV tunes, such as "The House Is Rockin'," from *In Step*.

Vaughan combines the influences of Chuck Berry and T-Bone Walker in his burning guitar solo (see **FIGURE 3**), and, in the second solo chorus, he plays a flashy lick based on chromatically ascending 6/9 chords. In the first three bars of this chorus, Vaughan repeatedly bends an A diminished voicing; this is a lick closely associated with T-Bone. Vaughan shifts to the chromatically-ascending

FIGURE 2

FIGURE 3

"Love Struck Baby" Guitar Solo

* Chord name derived from bass figure

* Fret ⑥ w/thumb

chords in bars 4 and 5.

On the return to A in bar 7, Vaughan incorporates a little voice-leading in his use of the A7add2 chord (this voicing is sometimes referred to as the "Hideaway" chord, for it is prominently featured in that Freddie King standard). Vaughan finishes off the chorus with a handful of standard Chuck Berry-isms, replete with sliding doublestops and triplestop bends.

One of Stevie Ray's best-loved tunes is another original from *Texas Flood*, "Pride and Joy." **FIGURE 4** illustrates the 16-bar intro from this classic tune, which is written in even or "straight" eighths, but is played with a "triplet feel." Bars 1 and 3 feature the unison high E notes, a signature of the tune, and, in bar 5, Vaughan launches into the rhythm guitar part of doom. To recreate this figure properly, use an alternating down-up-down-up strumming pattern throughout, catching the open top three strings on each upbeat (upstroke). These upstrokes should sound as percussive as possible, so, with the left hand, mute these open strings slightly for a more staccato attack. Aggressive right-hand strumming is a must, also.

In bars 13-16, Vaughan plays well-crafted single-note lines based on the E blues scale (E G A Bb B D) through the B7-A7-E7-B7 turnaround. The influence of blues pioneers Lightnin' Hopkins and Muddy Waters (plus a touch of blues/rock greats Jimi Hendrix and Johnny Winter) is in evidence with these classic licks.

The title cut from Vaughan's first album, a smoldering slow blues written by Fenton Robinson and recorded by Larry Davis during the Sixties, offered Stevie Ray the opportunity to let the world know just how much he could do with a slow blues. Vaughan's performance on this tune is riveting; you'd be hard-pressed to find a better example of focus and intensity in improvised blues guitar playing. Vaughan also used the tune to illustrate his love—and thorough assimilation—of the Albert King school of soloing, earmarked by precise microtonal bends and a stinging, fingerpicked attack.

FIGURE 5 illustrates a four-bar intro and five bars of soloing along the lines of the "Texas Flood" intro. The majority of the improvisation is based on G minor pentatonic (G Bb C D F), with a touch of the G blues scale thrown in (adding Db—the b5 of G—to the G minor pentatonic scale yields the G blues scale).

In bar 5 of this example (the actual beginning of the 12-bar form), the first note is sounded by fingerpicking: Hook the middle finger of your right hand under the string, and pick the note by

FIGURE 4

FIGURE 5

* chord names reflect overall tonality

* chord name derived from bass figure

† = pick note w/r.h. middle ringer, snapping string against fretboard.

pulling up and snapping the string against the fretboard. Vaughan is paying homage to blues great Albert King here, as this picking technique is essential to the Albert King sound and style. A symbol is used to indicate which notes should be picked in this manner.

At the end of a few phrases, such as the end of bars 5 and 9, Vaughan aggressively slides down the top three strings, fretting from no place in particular. Start somewhere near the end of the fretboard—from the 18th fret or higher—and fret the top three strings with a combination of your pinky and middle finger. The important thing here is the explosive sound Vaughan was looking for, not the specific notes that are fretted.

Another great cover tune from *Texas Flood* is "Mary Had a Little Lamb," a Buddy Guy classic originally cut by Buddy for his seminal 1968 album, *A Man and the Blues.* **FIGURE 6** illustrates this song's intro, on which Vaughan sticks very close to Buddy's original recording. Throughout this rhythm figure, Vaughan alternates, bar by bar, between chordal work and single-note lines, which are based on E minor pentatonic (E G A B D).

For the solo on this tune, Vaughan strung together three of the greatest choruses he ever played, in the creation of one truly great solo. It's all here: touch, tone, phrasing and feel—you just can't ask

FIGURE 6

"Mary Had a Little Lamb" Intro

for more. **FIGURE 7** illustrates nine bars of soloing along the lines of Vaughan's first solo. This solo, based also on E minor pentatonic, is impeccably phrased, and features fingerpicking, in bar 2, and cool half-step pre-bends in bars 5 and 8.

FIGURE 7

Like any master musician, Vaughan was just as comfortable with slow, delicate ballads as he was with barn burners. Vaughan composed the beautiful ballad, "Lenny," for his first wife, and recorded it on *Texas Flood*. "Lenny" is very Hendrix influenced; it's sort of a cross between "Little Wing" and "Angel," two of Hendrix's greatest ballads. Similar to "Mary Had a Little Lamb," Vaughan alternates between chords and single-note lines in bars 1-3. See **FIGURE 8**. The single-note lines here are based on E major pentatonic (E F# G# B C#).

Notice the use of "thumbed" root notes throughout (chords in which the root note on the low E string is fretted with the thumb), as well as the subtle bar vibratos added to most of the chords. In bars 5 through 8, be sure to allow all notes to sustain as long as possible. For more beautiful chord work in a ballad setting, check out "Riviera

FIGURE 8

Paradise," Vaughan's jazz-tinged original from *In Step*.

On Vaughan's second album, *Couldn't Stand the Weather*, Vaughan emerged as a rock songwriter to be reckoned with. Along with the powerful title track, the album also features the originals "Scuttle Buttin,' " "Honey Bee" and "Stang's Swang," plus the classic cut, "Cold Shot," written by keyboardist Mike Kendrid and arranged by SRV.

The title track opens with some free-time soloing over a Bm-A7-G7-F#7#9 chord progression, before settling into an r&b-based groove and a catchy single-note lick, played in unison by guitar and bass. This figure is illustrated in **FIGURE 9A**. Notice in particular the insertion of a 2/4 bar, at the beginning of the third ending.

For the next section, Vaughan introduces a flashy rhythm-

FIGURE 9

"Couldn't Stand the Weather"

A) Intro Lick

based figure which combines octaves, doublestops, thumbed bass notes and single-note figures. This highly mobile guitar part (see **FIGURE 9B**) indicates the influence of r&b guitarists such as Curtis Mayfield, Ike Turner, Bobby Womack and Don Covay on Vaughan. To recreate this part authentically, be sure to use alternate strumming in steady 16th notes throughout.

Our final example is the main figure from the fire-breathing tune "Scuttle Buttin'." About this tune, Stevie Ray said, "My brother Jimmie and I both know that 'Scuttle Buttin' ' is really just another way to play Lonnie Mack's 'Chicken Feed.' That's all it is." Still,

Lonnie never played with the *fury* Vaughan displays on this tune. The main lick, illustrated in **FIGURE 10**, is built from a fast, repeated lick based on the E blues scale (E G A Bb B D). The tune also features abundant use of an E7#9(no 3) chord, a chord Vaughan also credited to Lonnie Mack.

FIGURE 10

GUITAR WORLD, DECEMBER 1990

A HELLUVA BLUESMAN

Stevie Ray is remembered by his peers.

BUDDY GUY

"As a bluesman, he was as good as anybody. Ever."

NILE RODGERS (*Family Style* producer)

"David Bowie and I were doing the *Let's Dance* record in Switzerland, and this one day, David comes in raving about this amazing blues guitarist he'd just seen at the Montreaux Jazz Festival. He was just over the top about the guy, saying that he just had to have him on the record.

"I don't think Stevie had any thoughts that the recording would bring him fame or worldwide attention. He just came in with his guitar, put on the headphones, listened to what we'd been doing, smiled and said, 'Man, that sounds great!'

"Doing the record [*Family Style*] with Jimmie and Stevie years later was such a joy because the three of us felt so connected. I wanted the record to reflect how we enjoyed being together, so I asked them to keep the themes of the songs light and fun. I had to stress that to Stevie a couple of times: 'Don't write anything too heavy, Stevie, save that for later.' So what happens? Jimmie and I go and write 'Tick Tock,' which is a pretty heavy song. And on top of that we gave it to Stevie to sing! He thought that was pretty funny.

"As he was singing 'Tick Tock,' I was so thrilled to hear Stevie's warmth and compassion come through him as a vocalist. He was very shy about that, because it meant putting his guitar down and letting his voice do all the emoting. Weeks later, though, I listened to the song and became concerned that we didn't have his guitar on it, so I called him and said, 'Uh, Stevie, I think we need a little guitar from you on the song. Maybe just play little spots of notes, like B.B. King.' Stevie hopped on a plane and flew in to do literally 20 seconds of notes. What he played was so concise and dramatic, well, it just blew me away. That was the last thing he recorded for the record."

STEVE STEVENS

"I first became aware of him when I was working on Billy Idol's *Rebel Yell* album. Keith Forsey, who produced the album, came in with some advance tapes of David Bowie's *Let's Dance*. I was so taken with how great Bowie sounded with this American blues guitarist. It was such a great departure for David, who in the past had used players with an English sound.

"After *Let's Dance* appeared, I noticed how often producers and nonguitarists began to mention Stevie Ray; his sound and style became a real reference point for them. That's important, because so much of the time guitarists are the only ones who absorb what other players are doing. Stevie Ray's sound and aura appealed to everyone. The only other time I noticed that happening was with Hendrix.

"His style went beyond his incredible vibrato and masterful use of sound. His thinking was wide-open, and his playing naturally reflected that. You know, you always hear the same thing, how you almost have to go through hell to have the right to play the blues. I don't know if that's so true. But with Stevie Ray, who had indeed gone through so much, and had kicked alcoholism and drugs, it just couldn't be argued that when you heard him play, what you really heard was the man, playing his heart out. He just couldn't play a false note."

JESSE JOHNSON (The Time)

"The dude was funky. He'd be doing shit all through the song, throwing in solo fills, going back to rhythm, never leaving the groove. That always blew me away. That's what I like, when a cat can throw soul off like that. He was like B.B. and Albert King; when you go to see those cats, you know somebody's soul is gonna be crying that night."

WILL LEE (From *Late Night with David Letterman*'s CBS Orchestra)

"Musically, he was a powerhouse; the intensity of his playing would just blow you away. He'd create these deep, soulful pockets that I, as a bass player, would luxuriate in.

"The last time he played with us in New York, we played 'Crossfire.' But what really blew everyone away was when, during those little breaks we do before commercials, we went into Hendrix songs. Man, he played the shit out of those songs. He was on fire."

JEFF HEALEY

"In early 1983 I came home from a gig one evening to hear Stevie Ray Vaughan performing live, on the radio, from a Toronto club. He floored me. Here was a great player with a natural talent—and no pop rock crap. His performance that night convinced me that I should continue in the direction that I'd decided on for myself.

"I saw him the night before he died, and he was happier than I'd seen him for about five years. He was particularly excited about finally doing an album with Jimmie, who was not only his brother, but his idol as well."

DANNY GATTON

"The odds against someone like Stevie Ray Vaughan becoming successful in this business were so great. For years, blues was on the outside of marketing and radio. Stevie Ray opened the door for all of us.

"His style was so powerfully distinctive. You could literally hear three notes and know it was him. He got more sounds out of a Stratocaster than anybody, and his use of sound was absolutely masterful. And string-bending—he was the best! I think he used .012s on his E string, and man, he could bend that string like it was nothing. He was amazing.

"My big dream was to play with him. He was an incredible inspiration. I hope people keep listening to him forever."

GREGG ALLMAN

"What I always really admired about him was the stern kindness that he showed his band. They always came first; he always made sure their needs were taken care of. He loved those boys.

"He was a helluva bluesman. And a gentleman."

COLIN JAMES

"I had the opportunity to open for Stevie Ray when he did his first club tour of Canada. We got along real well, and I explained to him that I was having trouble keeping a band together and getting noticed in Canada. So he told me that Austin, Texas, was a better place to get something happening. So what did Stevie do? He took me down to Austin with him, put me up in a hotel and introduced me to everybody! He was so generous."

LONNIE MACK

"He was a giver—Stevie Ray was kind to everybody. If you were bad-mouthing somebody else, he wouldn't talk to you. My father always said, 'You can't put an old head on a young body,' but Stevie Ray Vaughan disproved that. That is why, despite the fact that he was much younger than I, we were friends—real friends. It went beyond guitar, to the heart and soul."

RONNIE EARL

"I ran into him just a few months after he had cleaned up. I was still using drugs and was pretty messed up. He didn't say anything about it to me then, but the next time I saw him, after I had left Roomful of Blues, we were both clean and he was very happy for me. That was the beginning of a very strong bond between us.

"Once, at the Great Woods Festival in Boston, he and his crew and I had a little one-day-at-a-time meeting in my dressing room.

That's when I really started seeing the spiritual side of Stevie. The last time I talked to him, I told him of some feelings of low self esteem I'd been having, and he told me that when you stop taking drugs, all your insecurities come out because you're so used to covering all that up and stuffing your feelings with drugs. 'Listen,' he said, 'whenever you're feeling down, call me. You have it harder than me because you're still playing in the bars, but you gotta just keep trying.'

"He was a beautiful person, very sincere, very human. I learned a lot from him and I'll carry it with me. I really miss him, and will probably be talking about him for the rest of my life."

Guitar World Presents is an ongoing series of books filled with the extraordinary interviews, feature pieces and instruction material that have made *Guitar World* magazine the world's most popular musicians' magazine. For years, *Guitar World* magazine has brought you the most timely, the most accurate and the most hard-hitting news and views about your favorite players. Now you can have it all in one convenient package: *Guitar World Presents*. The first four volumes of the series–Kiss, Van Halen, Metallica and Stevie Ray Vaughan–are here, ready to blow you away. Eddie Van Halen's fans have the opportunity to learn all about rock guitar's resident genius–straight from his mouth. Are you a Kiss fan who wants the full story behind the band's incredible 1996 reunion tour? No problem–it's all in *Guitar World Presents*, as are Stevie Ray Vaughan's tragedies and triumphs and Metallica's march to the top.

Prepare yourself. *Guitar World Presents*–the books that rock.

Guitar World Presents Kiss

From the pages of *Guitar World* magazine, the foremost musicians' publication in America, comes *Guitar World Presents Kiss*, an exciting and often explosive collection of interviews, articles and essays on rock's most famous masked marauders. In-depth conversations with band members Gene Simmons, Paul Stanley, Ace Frehley and Peter Criss chronicle the entire history of Kiss, from the band's modest beginnings in New York City to their incredible rise to international prominence, subsequent collapse and triumphant comeback on their 1996 reunion tour. Devoted Kiss fans and recent converts alike will find *Guitar World Presents Kiss* to be one book they really can't do without. Includes Photos.
Soft cover, 6"x9"–144 pages, $12.95.....00330291

Guitar World Presents Metallica

More than any other publication, *Guitar World* magazine has followed Metallica's rise from underground phenomenon to mainstream metal giant. *Guitar World Presents Metallica* features every one of the facts and figures, interviews and stories, about the band ever to have appeared in the magazine in one self-contained package. Presented in the chronological order in which they appeared in the magazine, the revealing interviews with band members James Hetfield, Kirk Hammett, Jason Newsted and Lars Ulrich tell the story of the boys from San Francisco who went on to become the metal men of the world. Metallica fans will find everything they ever wanted to know about their heavy metal heroes right here in *Guitar World Presents Metallica*. Includes photos.
Soft Cover, 6"x9"–144 pages, $12.95.....00330292

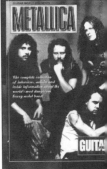

Guitar World Presents Van Halen

No artist has ever been more closely associated with *Guitar World* magazine over the years than Edward Van Halen, the man who, in the late seventies and early eighties, changed the course of guitar history. This collection of classic interviews with the great Edward tells the real story behind his earth-shaking technique, brilliant songwriting and relationships with Van Halen's former vocalists, David Lee Roth and Sammy Hagar. This is the authoritative book about the age's seminal rock guitar god. Includes photos.
Soft Cover, 6"x9"–208 pages, $14.95.....00330294

Guitar World Presents Stevie Ray Vaughan

Stevie Ray Vaughan, bluesman, guitarist and legend, was only 35 at the time of his death, but in his lifetime he managed to revitalize the blues, influence a generation of guitarists and produce a phenomenal body of work. His story is told here in *Guitar World Presents Stevie Ray Vaughan*, a collection of articles about the great guitarist from the pages of *Guitar World* magazine. This deluxe volume features probing interviews held over the years with Stevie Ray, instructional material, a complete discography of his recorded works and living reminiscences by his fellow musicians. *Guitar World Presents Stevie Ray Vaughan* is an essential tribute to a great fallen guitar hero of our generation. Includes photos.
Soft Cover, 6"x9"–144 pages, $12.95 00330293

DOUBLE WHAMMY!

SUBSCRIBE NOW AND GET 'EM BOTH!

Play the Music of Stevie Ray Vaugha

WITH AUTHENTIC, NOTE-FOR-NOTE GUITAR TRANSCRIPTIONS FROM HAL LEONA

ALL BOOKS INCLUDE NOTES AND TABLATURE.

COULDN'T STAND THE WEATHER

Matching folio includes the title song and: Scuttle Buttin' • Things That I Used To Do • Voodoo Child (Slight Return) • Cold Shot • and more. Also includes photos.

00690024 Guitar Recorded Versions.... $19.95

LIVE ALIVE

Matching folio, including: Look At Little Sister • Love Struck Baby • Mary Had A Little Lamb • Pride And Joy • Superstition • Voodoo Chile • and more.

Includes photos.

00690036 Guitar Recorded Versions.... $24.95

BIG BL FROM TEXAS

by Dave K

Learn the licks and n selected Stevie R greatest Each so explained analyzed through in-depth lessons and tr tions.

00660045 Guitar School . . . .

IN STEP

Matching folio with 10 songs, including: The House Is Rockin' • Crossfire • Tightrope • Let Me Love You Baby • Love Me Darlin' • and more.

00660136 Guitar Recorded Versions.... $19.95
00694777 Bass Recorded Versions..... $14.95

THE SKY IS CRYING

Matching folio to the album featuring 10 previously unreleased studio performances, including: The Sky Is Crying • Empty Arms • Little Wing • Life By The Drop • and more.

00694835 Guitar Recorded Versions.... $19.95

SRV GU COLLEC

24 songs, ing: Stand Weather Struck Ba Without Empty Arr House Is • Pride A

Scuttle Buttin' • So Excited • and more

00690116 Guitar Recorded Versions. . .

IN THE BEGINNING

Matching folio to the recording of the first-ever, live radio broadcast by SRV and Double Trouble from April 1, 1980. 10 songs, including: They Call Me Guitar Hurricane • Tin Pan Alley • Love Struck Baby • Live Another Day • and more.

00694879 Guitar Recorded Versions.... $19.95

SOUL TO SOUL

10-song matching folio includes: Say What • Look At Little Sister • Ain't Gone 'N' Give Up On Love • Change It • You'll Be Mine • Empty Arms • Life Without You.

00690025 Guitar Recorded Versions $19.95

SIGNA LICKS

by Wolf Marshal

An explora this genius. explaine influenc ing, eq picking technique and other as Vaughan's sound. In addition, he tr parts of 13 of Vaughan's most famous s explains how they were played and wh them so unique. 59-minute accompan

00699316 Guitar-Book/CD Pack . . . . . .

TEXAS FLOOD

Matching folio with 10 songs, including: I'm Cryin • Lenny • Love Struck Baby • Pride And Joy • and more.

00690015 Guitar Recorded Versions.... $19.95

Prices, contents and availability subject to change without notice.
Some products may not be available outside the U.S.A.